TABLE

OUTLINE FOR THE PSALMS

LESSON ONE: HYMNS OF PRAISE
  Psalms 8, 19, 29, 33, 47, 93, 95, 96, 97, 98, 99, 104
LESSON TWO: HYMNS OF PRAISE
  Psalms 113, 114, 115, 117, 121, 134, 135, 145, 146, 147, 148, 149, 150
LESSON THREE: SONGS OF ZION
  Psalms 15, 24, 46, 48, 76, 84, 87, 122, 132
LESSON FOUR: ROYAL PSALMS
  Psalms 2, 18, 20, 21, 45, 72, 89, 101, 110, 144
LESSON FIVE: COMMUNAL THANKSGIVING PSALMS
  Psalms 65, 66, 67, 75, 100, 105, 106, 107, 124, 136
LESSON SIX: INDIVIDUAL THANKSGIVING PSALMS
  Psalms 30, 32, 34, 40, 41, 92, 103, 111, 116, 118, 138
LESSON SEVEN: INDIVIDUAL LAMENTS
  Psalms 3, 4, 5, 6, 7, 9, 10, 13, 14, 17, 22, 25
LESSON EIGHT: INDIVIDUAL LAMENTS
  Psalms 26, 27, 28, 31, 35, 36, 38, 39, 42, 43, 51, 52, 53
LESSON NINE: INDIVIDUAL LAMENTS
  Psalms 54, 55, 56, 57, 58, 59, 61, 63, 64, 69, 70, 71, 77
LESSON TEN: INDIVIDUAL LAMENTS
  Psalms 86, 88, 94, 102, 108, 109, 120, 130, 139, 140, 141, 142, 143
LESSON ELEVEN: COMMUNAL LAMENTS
  Psalms 12, 44, 60, 74, 79, 80, 83, 85, 90, 123, 125, 126, 129, 137
LESSON TWELVE: WISDOM PSALMS
  Psalms 1, 37, 49, 73, 78, 91, 112, 119, 127, 128, 133
LESSON THIRTEEN: PSALMS OF CONFIDENCE
  Psalms 11, 16, 23, 62, 131
  MISCELLANEOUS PSALMS
  Psalms 50, 68, 81, 82

*O LORD, our Lord, / how majestic
is your name in all the earth! (8:1).*

—— 1 ——
Hymns of Praise

• • •

DIMENSION ONE:
WHAT DOES THE BIBLE SAY?

Answer these questions by reading Psalm 8

1. The psalm talks to whom? (8:1)

2. What has God created? (8:3)

3. How are human beings described in the psalm? (8:4-5)

Answer these questions by reading Psalm 19

4. What is proclaiming God's glory in the psalm? (19:1)

5. How does the psalmist describe God's law? (19:7-9)

6. What must our words and thoughts be in relationship to God? (19:14)

Answer these questions by reading Psalm 29

7. The psalm talks to whom? (29:1)

8. What does the voice of God do? (29:3-9)

9. What does the psalmist ask from God? (29:11)

Answer these questions by reading Psalm 33

10. Who should praise God according to his psalm? (33:1)

11. How should God be praised? (33:2-3)

12. What does God do? (33:13-14)

13. What makes the psalmist glad? (33:20-21)

Answer these questions by reading Psalm 47

14. Who is asked to praise God? (47:1)

15. Why should God be praised? (47:7)

Answer these questions by reading Psalm 96

16. What kind of song does the psalmist want us to sing to God? (96:1)

17. Why should we sing to God? (96:4-5)

18. What should we tell the nations about God? (96:10)

Answer these questions by reading Psalm 104

19. Where do we find the clearest evidence of God's work in the world? (104:10, 14, 24)

20. How long will the psalmist praise God? (104:33)

DIMENSION TWO:
WHAT DOES THE BIBLE MEAN?

The hymns of praise covered in this lesson are Psalms 8, 19, 29, 33, 96, and 104. Psalms 47, 93, 95, 97, 98, and 99 are of the same type, but are not examined here. All the hymns of praise in the Book of Psalms begin with an introductory call to worship. This call to worship is either a call for others to praise God or for the psalmist to do so (see Psalm 8:1). Next the reason for praise is given. Why should we praise God? (See Psalm 8:5-8.) Finally a summary act of praise is given. This follows a renewed call to praise (see Psalm 8:9).

Now let us look in more detail at some of these hymns of praise we have read.

❏ *Psalm 8:1.* The New International Version (NIV) translates the Hebrew consonants YHWH as "Lord." Often this word is written in English as *Yahweh. Yahweh* is the distinctive name of the Hebrew God, revealed to Moses in Exodus 3:14. Note that Yahweh's name is everywhere, "in all the earth."

❏ *Psalm 8:2.* Though Yahweh is "above the heavens," Yahweh's glory comes from the lips of the most inarticulate and unexpected persons in creation, "children and infants."

❏ *Psalm 8:3-8.* The sight of Yahweh's creation, "the heavens" (or more clearly in Hebrew, "the sky") and "the moon and the stars" causes the psalmist to be amazed by the insignificance of humanity and by God's interest in and care for humanity. Human beings are puny and yet "little lower than the heavenly beings." They are given sweeping power by God over God's creation.

The word translated *man* in the NIV is more correctly translated *humanity.*

❏ *Psalm 8:9.* After these great thoughts about God and humanity, the psalmist can only repeat the word of praise that began the psalm.

❏ *Psalm 19:1-6.* God's creation shouts God's praise without the use of words. The sun, from whose heat nothing can hide, is God's greatest physical creation of the sky. Just like God, the sun is everywhere and the very source of life.

❑ **Psalm 19:7-11.** The psalmist shifts suddenly to a discussion of God's law (a translation of the Hebrew word *torah*). God is not revealed only in the physical creation. God's teaching provides needed boundaries to life and provides the rewards of servanthood (verse 11).

❑ **Psalm 19:14.** The psalmist's last humble plea is that all words and acts may be finally acceptable to God, this great creator God of power and law.

❑ **Psalm 29:1.** The psalm is addressed to "mighty ones." In Hebrew this literally means *the sons of gods.* This very old psalm refers to a divine court of many gods with Yahweh as their chief. The idea of and belief in only one God was developed over a long period of time. See Job 1–2 and Exodus 20:3 for other examples in the Old Testament of a belief in the existence of many gods.

❑ **Psalm 29:3-9.** The imagery of a thunderstorm provides the description of God's presence here. Notice the thundering voice (verse 3), the flashing fire (verse 7), and the howling wind (verse 9).

❑ **Psalm 29:11.** The psalm begins (verse 1) by asking the sons of god to praise the strength of Yahweh. The psalm ends by asking Yahweh to give strength to the people. But not just strength is requested. Strength should always be accompanied by peace, *shalom. Shalom* in Hebrew comes from the root word for *unity.* It means "wholeness, oneness."

❑ **Psalm 33:1.** The words *righteous* and *upright* of verse 1 come originally from the language of a court of law. In the Old Testament, persons are righteous and upright if they fulfill responsibilities in relationships to others. These terms always refer to people in community, not people by themselves.

❑ **Psalm 33:4.** Notice that because God's word is "right and true," those who are "righteous" and "upright" (verse 1) are called to praise God.

❑ **Psalm 33:6-9.** Once again the creation of the world is seen as God's great act. Notice the relationship of verse 9 to the Creation story of Genesis 1.

❑ **Psalm 33:20-21.** Praise is appropriate because we trust the past, present, and future activity of God.

❏ *Psalm 47:1-2.* This psalm emphasizes the universal praise of God. All nations (verse 1) are called to praise "the great King over all the earth" (verse 2; see also verse 7).

❏ *Psalm 96:1.* The hymns of praise often call for a "new song" (96:1; 33:3; 98:1; Isaiah 42:10). God's ever-new activity on behalf of the people requires new ways of praise.

❏ *Psalm 96:10.* The word *equity* is from the same Hebrew word that was earlier transcribed as *upright.* God is upright and demands the same from the people. As God deals with equity so must you and I deal equitably with our brothers and sisters.

❏ *Psalm 104:24.* Once again the physical creation is the clearest sign of God's work.

DIMENSION THREE:
WHAT DOES THE BIBLE MEAN TO ME?

These hymns of praise raise two ideas that are meaningful for us today.

Psalm 8—GOD Is the Creator of All

In most of the hymns of praise we see that God's creation of the physical universe—sun, moon, stars, mountains, trees, water, plants, and humanity—is the chief reason why we should sing praises. These psalms simply assume that God created all life. Note that the psalmist does not argue about how God did it, the psalmist asserts that God did it and then praises God for it.

In our time a huge debate is taking place about the means and the time of creation—did creation occur ten billion years ago or ten thousand years ago? Is evolution responsible for all life on earth, or did all living things simply appear as they now are? As interesting as these questions are, they are not the questions of the Bible. The Bible and these psalms simply say, "God is the creator of all things." And for that God is worthy to be praised. To believe God is creator of all is not to deny or affirm either creationism or evolution. The belief in God as creator begins in faith and grows in faith. How do you relate a belief in God as creator to your views about science?

When we affirm that God is creator of all, we also affirm that God owns all and has a claim on all. If God is creator, then nothing else or no one else is. So God is the only being worthy of ultimate concern and ultimate praise. If we praise the creator God, there can be no place for the ultimate praise of any secondary creator, any man or woman, any group or society or nation. To praise God as creator is to get our priorities straight, to put God in the center of creation, and to push everything and everyone else off center. That is why it is so important that our most-used creeds, such as the Apostles' and the Nicene, affirm God as creator in their first lines. Is a belief in God as creator of all important to you? Why or why not? Try to tell another class member about your belief in God as creator.

Psalm 19—God Is the Creator of ALL

The hymns of praise often use universal language when speaking of God's creation (see Psalm 96:1, 7). The first affirmation of Genesis 1, "In the beginning God created the heavens and the earth," speaks of the universality of God. If God creates all, then God loves all, and God deals with all in equity, justice, and righteousness.

Psalm 19 is especially helpful at this point. The psalm begins by describing the universal creation of God. God's most amazing created thing is the sun, whose heat is given to all (verse 6). The psalmist implies that God is like the sun in that no one hides from God. But because God created the sun, God is greater than the sun. The psalm does not just say "Praise God, because God created the physical universe." God also creates *torah*, or the law and teaching, which God then gives to all for ordering their lives on earth.

That God's *torah* is more than a set of laws to follow is made clear by the psalm. Verses 7-9 offer five words to help clarify the meaning of *torah*. They are *law, statutes, precepts, commands,* and *ordinances. Torah* is literally what God has given to us and what we do in response to that gift.

Because God creates *torah* and offers it to all, we can never look at one another the same way again. Each of us is a created child of God, and a recipient of God's *torah*. Each of us is at the same time a tiny speck in the vast ocean of God's universe (Psalm 8:3-4) and "little less than the heavenly beings" (Psalm 8:5). We are at once dependent and powerful, paltry and magnificent, tiny and titanic.

To believe in God as creator of all is to believe in the "Godlikeness" of each human being. What a revolutionary idea! All our easy labels are torn off! When God is creator of all, I must be related to all and concerned about all, and not just in an abstract way. Every human being is included in God's "all" and so must be in my "all" as well. Is this a freeing concept of God as creator of all or a threatening one for you? How can you make the connection between God as creator and your love of God's creation? What stands in your way?

*From the rising of the sun to the place
where it sets, / the name of the LORD is to be praised (113:3).*

2

Hymns of Praise

• • •

DIMENSION ONE:
WHAT DOES THE BIBLE SAY?

Answer these questions by reading Psalm 113

1. Where does the psalmist say that God is? (113:4)

2. Why is God worthy of praise? (113:7-9)

3. The psalm begins and ends with what words? (113:1, 9)

Answer these questions by reading Psalm 114

4. What is missing from the beginning of this hymn of praise? (114:1)

5. What great events of Israel's past form the basis for this psalm? (114:1-8)

6. What is missing at the end of this hymn of praise? (114:8)

Answer these questions by reading Psalm 121

7. How is the mood of Psalm 121 different from that of Psalm 113?

8. How is God described in this psalm? (121:2, 4, 5)

9. How are the endings of Psalm 121 and Psalm 113 different? (113:9 and 121:8)

Answer these questions by reading Psalm 135

10. Who are asked to praise God in this psalm? (135:1-2)

11. Which actions of God are praised here? (135:6-12)

12. Who are called on to praise the Lord? (135:19-20)

Answer these questions by reading Psalm 145

13. How does the psalmist describe God's greatness? (145:3)

14. How else is God described in this psalm? (145:8)

15. In whom is God especially interested? (145:14)

Answer these questions by reading Psalm 146

16. How long will the psalmist praise God? (146:2)

17. Why should we not trust in princes? (146:3-4)

18. To whom does God show special care? (146:7-9)

Answer these questions by reading Psalm 150

19. Where should God be praised? (150:1)

20. Why should God be praised? (150:2)

21. How should God be praised? (150:3-5)

22. Who should praise God? (150:6)

DIMENSION TWO:
WHAT DOES THE BIBLE MEAN?

The hymns of praise covered in this lesson are Psalms 113, 114, 121, 135, 145, 146, and 150. Psalms 115, 117, 134, 147, 148, and 149 are psalms of the same type, but are not examined here. Lesson 1 pointed out that all the hymns of praise follow a general threefold pattern. As is often the case in biblical studies, this generalization has exceptions. Psalm 114 clearly does not follow the pattern.

The Bible is diverse in outlook and scope. One cannot make easy statements about "what it says." All of us should remember this fact in a day when the Bible is used by some as a stick to break over the heads of "evildoers." In such cases, the "evil-doers" are so labeled by those who wield the club.

The Book of Psalms is one of the Bible's best witnesses to diversity in outlook. Even though Psalm 114 does not fit the expected pattern, it is just as certainly a psalm of praise.

❑ *Psalm 113:1.* The psalm opens with the phrase, "Praise the LORD" or *Hallelujah.* Literally, this English word is two Hebrew words that mean Praise Yah! The word *praise* is a plural command form, while *Yah* is the short form of one of the Hebrew words for God, *Yahweh.* (See the discussion of Psalm 8:1 in Lesson 1.)

❑ *Psalm 113:5-6.* God is often pictured in the psalms as "enthroned on high," "high up," "above the sky." This metaphor of God up high has sometimes been taken too literally by well-meaning Christians. They limit their understandings of God as one who lives "up there" and/or "out there." Other places in the Scripture break through this overly simple view. Psalm 139 speaks of God as absolutely everywhere. And the prophet Amos, quoting this same tradition, affirms the same truth (Amos 9:2-3). First Kings 8:27 suggests that "the heavens, even the highest heaven, cannot contain you." To limit God to a single place is to make God too small.

❑ *Psalm 113:7-9.* God's great exaltation above and beyond the created world is once again contrasted with God's special care for the world (see Psalm 8). God especially cares for the lowest members of society. This theme is of nearly universal interest for the authors of the Bible. God is particularly interested in the poor, the needy, and the barren. God searches for ways to right the inequalities of God's creatures. The poor and needy will sit with princes, and the barren woman will receive a home. (See 1 Samuel 2:4-8 and Luke 1:48-53.)

❑ *Psalm 114:1.* This psalm does not have a call to worship, nor is there a call to praise at the end. All eight verses glorify the great work of God in the Exodus experience. We hear of the escape from Egypt (verse 1), and God's provision of water in the desert (verse 8). In between, earthquake imagery adds to the picture of God's power over nations and nature.

❑ *Psalm 121:1.* Psalm 121 is one of the most familiar hymns of praise. It, like Psalm 114, does not follow the pattern of a typical psalm of praise. There is no call to worship or call to praise at the end. The mood seems noticeably different as well. No shouts for praise. No great exclamations of God's power. The psalmist seems quiet, almost contemplative. In the first verse there is a fascinating use of the traditional and the surprising. "I lift up my eyes to the hills," the psalmist begins. One could reasonably expect to find God there. After all, Sinai is a hill where God was found. But our psalmist goes on to ask a probing question: "Where does my help come from?" Not from the hills. Real help comes from "the LORD, the Maker of heaven and earth," which obviously includes the hills.

❑ *Psalm 121:3, 4, 5 7, 8.* Note how the word *watch* is repeated in the psalm. This word in Hebrew means guard and protect as well as possess or hold on to. The psalmist wants to affirm that we are God's possession always (verse 8). We will be protected by God always (verses 7-8). Such quiet comfort and such powerful certainty!

❑ *Psalm 135:1-2.* This psalm is particularly directed to the priests, those special guardians of the traditions, house, and laws of God. They are the ones who "minister in the house of the LORD," and in the "courts of the house of our God."

❑ *Psalm 135:7-12.* Here we get a miniature history of Israel from Creation (verse 7) to the Promised Land (verse 12). For all of these great deeds, God is worthy of praise.

HYMNS OF PRAISE

❏ **Psalm 135:19-20.** Here the priests are named as members of the house of Aaron and Levi, the traditional priestly houses in Israel.

❏ **Psalm 145.** This psalm is an acrostic poem. In an acrostic poem each line begins with a letter of the Hebrew alphabet in order, from the first letter, *aleph*, to the final letter, *taw*. It is not quite a perfect acrostic, however, because a line beginning with the Hebrew letter *nun* is not in the poem. Perhaps it has fallen out accidentally. Translating the poem into English to retain the acrostic game that is being played would be virtually impossible. Such an acrostic poem was no doubt a good memory aid.

❏ **Psalm 145:3.** The psalmist, in praising God, momentarily runs out of words and simply affirms that God's greatness is such that "no one can fathom." No human language or effort can plumb the well of God. (See also Job 38.)

❏ **Psalm 145:8.** Here the psalmist quotes a very famous statement about the nature of God. See Exodus 34:6, Nehemiah 9:17, and Jonah 4:2 for this description of God.

❏ **Psalm 145:14-15.** Again God is particularly interested in those who are in special need of help, those who are falling, and those who are bowed down. But the psalmist quickly affirms that the eyes of everyone and everything look to God. God may have special concern for the poor and lowly. But at the same time God also has concern for the whole world that should turn to God in all things.

❏ **Psalm 146:2-3.** The psalmist vows to praise God as long as he is alive. This vow is in sharp contrast to the princes of the next verse who control the world only as long as they are alive. When they die all of their grandiose plans die with them. God, on the contrary, is the "Maker of heaven and earth" and "remains faithful forever" (verse 6).

❏ **Psalm 146:7-9.** Once again God's special concern is directed toward the powerless. Eight typical cases of Old Testament outcasts are listed: the oppressed, the hungry, prisoners, the blind, the bowed down, the alien, widows, and orphans. These represent a biblical "who's who" of those cast off by society but called righteous (verse 8) by God. This list reminds each of us to be alert to the actions of God in unexpected places and with unexpected people.

❑ *Psalm 150.* No more fitting psalm than Psalm 150 could be chosen to conclude the Book of Psalms. This psalm answers the four most basic questions about God's praise: where, why, how, and who.

❑ *Psalm 150:1.* God is praised in the sanctuary and in the world outside of the sanctuary, that is, everywhere.

❑ *Psalm 150:2.* God is praised for God's deeds. These deeds are manifestations of God's greatness.

❑ *Psalm 150:3-4.* God must be praised with every instrument of music available. This list of instruments might also indicate the kind of instruments that accompanied the psalms when they were recited in ancient Israel.

❑ *Psalm 150:6.* Everything that breathes should praise God. The whole Book of Psalms closes with the general command to "praise Yah!"

DIMENSION THREE:
WHAT DOES THE BIBLE MEAN TO ME?

Psalm 121—Where Can I See God at Work Today?

How can I know and affirm that God is active in my life and in our world now? For some of you, your belief in the actions of God recorded in the Bible are sufficient for you to affirm that fact. Indeed, the second part of the Book of Isaiah takes this same approach. If you believe God created the world, then surely you must believe that God is still interested in that world now. (See Isaiah 45:12-25, for example.)

But others of you might ask why God could not offer to you just one small miracle to prove God's presence. Perhaps God could produce a minor healing, a still small voice, or a special sign.

Psalm 121 speaks to this concern in a unique way. The psalmist states, "I lift up my eyes to the hills." The psalmist asks a serious and probing question. Do the hills provide help? The answer is quickly given that only God provides help.

When you remember that the Canaanites worshiped on high places, it could be that the psalmist is calling the worshipers to a new view of God. High places are magnetic in their appeal, but tend to create familiar expectations on the part of worshipers. Is God only in the hills? No, says our psalmist. Does the psalmist try to prove God's activity in life? No. The psalm quite simply affirms God's presence. God is the watcher, the sustainer, the ever-vigilant help for now and forever (verse 8).

A story about Jesus makes the point well (John 20:24-29). Thomas said he would believe that his master had been resurrected only when he could see and touch him for himself. Jesus appears and offers Thomas exactly that chance. Immediately Thomas cries out in loud confession, "My Lord and my God!" I always picture Jesus at this point with a rather wry grin on his face as he says, "Because you have seen me, you have believed; blessed are those who have not seen and yet have believed." Real faith needs no proof. The power of God is seen by those who have the eyes to see it. Do not look to the hills where others look. God can best be seen in unexpected ways. Where is God best seen in your life? Describe your experience with God to someone else in the class.

Psalms 113:7-9; 145:14; 146:7-9
God Is the God of the Powerless

Again and again in these psalms of praise we note that God is uniquely concerned with the lesser members of the psalmist's society. Psalms 113:7-9, 145:14, and 146:7-9 all say directly that God is on the side of those who have special needs.

Throughout the Bible God is presented to us as the God of the oppressed. But the oppressed can become the oppressors. Jeremiah upbraids his own people, former Egyptian slaves, for their oppression of the poor. He reminds King Jehoiakim that his father, Josiah, was "right and just." He suggests Josiah "defended the cause of the poor and the needy," an example of righteousness. Then Jeremiah drives home his point. "Is that not what it means to know me [God]?" (Jeremiah 22:16). God is best known when we are just and righteous.

In 1 John 4:20 we read that people who say "I love God" and hate their brothers or sisters are liars. And, of course the great parable of the Last Judgment of Matthew 25 (verses 31-46) should be remembered: "Whatever you did for one of the least of these brothers of mine, you did for me" (Matthew 25:40).

God is known by God's care for the poor, and God is best served by our care for those same poor. The Bible's message at this point seems clear and unequivocal.

But, Psalm 145:15 also says that the eyes of all look to God. God loves and cares for all, the oppressed and the oppressor. The Bible's message here is equally clear and unequivocal. What then are we to do? We, like God, must love all. We, like God, must especially love those who most need our love. God's special desire for the creation is harmony where all are equal in God's sight. This is made clear both at the beginning of the Bible (Genesis 1) and at the end (Revelation 22:1-5). God's search for this harmony must be matched by our own search. Our love of and work for the powerless moves our world closer to the one God intended in creation and intends forever.

Is this biblical message of God's love for the powerless new to you? How does it liberate you? How does it frighten you? Do you agree with it or disagree with it? Why?

*LORD, who may dwell in your
sanctuary? / Who may live on your holy hill? (15:1).*

——— 3 ———
Songs of Zion

• • •

DIMENSION ONE:
WHAT DOES THE BIBLE SAY?

Answer these questions by reading Psalm 15

1. What does the psalmist mean by "your sanctuary"? (15:1)

2. How does one gain entrance to the holy hill? (15:2-5)

Answer these questions by reading Psalm 24

3. What belongs to the Lord? (24:1)

4. Who is able to stand in God's holy place? (24:4)

5. Who is the King of glory? (24:8, 10)

Answer these questions by reading Psalm 46

6. How can we survive in a fast-changing world? (46:1)

7. Where does God dwell? (46:4)

8. What are the works of the Lord? (46:9)

Answer these questions by reading Psalm 48

9. Why is God to be praised? (48:4-8)

10. What is the task given to each reader of the psalm? (48:12-14)

Answer these questions by reading Psalm 76

11. What is "Salem" in this psalm? (76:2)

12. What is God's great work? (76:3, 5-6, 9)

13. What does God do to the rulers and kings of the earth? (76:12)

Answer these questions by reading Psalm 84

14. Where is God's dwelling place? (84:7)

15. How is God described in this psalm? (84:2, 3, 7, 11)

Answer these questions by reading Psalm 122

16. What is Jerusalem's role in this psalm? (122:3-4)

17. Is Jerusalem the main concern of the psalm? (122:9)

DIMENSION TWO:
WHAT DOES THE BIBLE MEAN?

The psalms covered in this lesson are Psalms 15, 24, 46, 48, 76, 84, and 122. Psalms 87 and 132 are also Songs of Zion, but are not examined here.

These nine psalms are grouped together because of a common general theme. They all refer to Zion, Jerusalem, God's Holy City. They are still hymns of praise, but it is Zion that is praised most directly. And Zion is seen as worthy of praise precisely because God has done and will do great things there. The name "Songs of Zion" comes from Psalm 137:3.

Zion as a name first appears in the narratives that tell about how David conquered Jerusalem (2 Samuel 5:6-10). Jerusalem is an old name of the pre-Israelite Jebusite city that was located in that area. David conquered the city and renamed it the city of David. All three names, Zion, Jerusalem, and the city of David, appear to refer to the same place in the later traditions. As these Zion psalms will demonstrate, the sacred place of Zion takes on great meaning for the Israelite psalmists. The meaning of Zion for the psalmists far transcends a mere hill or sanctuary.

❑ *Psalm 15:1.* This psalm is obviously a worship service in itself. It has been called an "entrance liturgy." The question is, Who has the right to enter the holy sanctuary of God? The sanctuary is also called here God's "holy hill." The answer to the question, probably asked by the priests, is given by the worshipers or perhaps by pilgrims who have come from far away to worship God in the great central shrine in Jerusalem. The use of the word *sanctuary* reminds us of the Tent of Meeting that was used by the Israelites during their wandering in the desert. The Tent of Meeting was a kind of portable church. (See Exodus 33:7-11 and Numbers 2:2.)

❑ *Psalm 15:2-5.* These verses give the requirements for anyone who wants to enter God's house. He or she must "walk blamelessly" (always obey God), act righteously, and speak the truth. These very general stipulations are then made more specific in verses 3-5. To enter God's house, persons must not slander anyone, hurt, or bring shame to a neighbor. They should honor all who worship God, and they should keep their vows. They cannot loan money at interest (see Exodus 22:25; Leviticus 25:35-37) or take bribes at the expense of the innocent.

Each of these seven requirements is quite basic to the operation of a just and equitable society. We should again note that these requirements are to be fulfilled before entrance into the sanctuary is granted.

❑ *Psalm 15:5.* The person who does all these things "will never be shaken" or will never deviate from the right path.

❑ *Psalm 24.* This psalm is quite similar to the preceding one as it also is an entrance liturgy for worshipers or pilgrims. Some scholars have suggested that the movement of the ark of the covenant to Jerusalem is the setting for the recital of this psalm.

❑ *Psalm 24:1-2.* The poem begins with a short recitation of the creative ownership of God. The words are used here to base the later demands of God squarely on God's creative power. The God who seeks worship and awe is the same God who owns the very earth that God "founded" and "established." The psalmist argues that if you believe God created the world, you should also believe that God's demands of you are to be taken seriously.

❑ *Psalm 24:3-4.* Verse 3 is very similar to Psalm 15:1. Also, the answer to the question is similar to Psalm 15:2-5. It begins with a general statement of the requirements for entrance: those with "clean hands" and "a pure heart." Then follow two more specific stipulations. The worshiper must not follow an idol or "swear by what is false." In other words, falsehood is ruled out for a worshiper of God. Truth and honesty rest at the very heart of any just society.

❑ *Psalm 24:6.* The kinds of people mentioned in verse 4 are precisely the kinds who seek entrance to the place of God, who seek "your face, O God of Jacob."

❑ *Psalm 24:7-10.* These words, made famous by Handel's *Messiah*, are merely a command that the sanctuary be opened to the worshipers. These worshipers are preceded inside by the "King of glory," none other than the "Lord Almighty."

❑ *Psalm 24:6, 10.* The meaning of the word *Selah* remains unknown to us. Possibly it calls for voices to be raised to a higher tone or pitch. It also might suggest an orchestral interlude or call for a change of voices within the choir. Another possibility is that it directs the worshipers to repeat a section of the poem such as verses 1-2 as a refrain. But none of these suggestions has conclusive proof to support it.

❑ *Psalm 46:1.* This verse inspired Martin Luther to write his powerful hymn, "A Mighty Fortress Is Our God." That hymn expresses well the sentiment of this song of Zion. Because God is "a bulwark never failing" we have no fear, even though a great cataclysm should strike the earth and the seas boil and foam out of their bed.

❑ *Psalm 46:4-6.* In contrast to the boiling seas, there is a "river whose streams make glad the city of God." This river, a magic stream connected to the holy city of Jerusalem, can be seen also in Isaiah 33:20-21, Ezekiel 47:1-12, Zechariah 14:8, and Revelation 22:1-2. In all these cases the river of Jerusalem refers to a new day for Jerusalem, a future Jerusalem where only God will reign. Even while the "nations are in uproar" and "kingdoms fall," God's voice is in control.

❑ *Psalm 46:8-9.* These will be God's great deeds for the future Jerusalem. The nations may be "in uproar," but "the desolations [God] has brought on the earth" are the destruction of bows, spears, and shields, so that wars will cease. God's peaceful kingdom, centered in Zion, is reminiscent of Isaiah 2:4.

❑ *Psalm 46:10.* God commands that the nations cease their squabbling and raging. God alone is exalted.

❑ *Psalm 48.* As in the preceding psalm, Psalm 48 describes the permanence of Zion, God's special blessing for it, and God's perpetual desire to maintain it through divine power.

❑ *Psalm 48:2.* Mount Zion, the home of the God of Israel, is "the joy of the whole earth" and thus greater than any other divine mountain.

❑ *Psalm 48:4-8.* God has defended Zion and will defend Zion against all destruction. Any would-be invaders are terrified and put to flight. Even huge ocean-going ships from Tarshish are shattered in a gale. (See 1 Kings 10:22.) God has established Zion forever and God is to be praised.

❑ *Psalm 48:12-14.* All worshipers are commanded to survey the great city by walking around it. Then they are to proclaim to the next generation that God is indeed protecting the city and will protect them.

❑ *Psalm 76:2.* "Salem" is apparently a short form for Jerusalem (see Genesis 14:18).

❑ *Psalm 76:3-5.* As in Psalm 46:9, God is praised here for the destruction of the weapons of war. Those who would come to make war on Zion find themselves incapable of battle. First, their arrows, shields, and swords are broken by God. Then they miraculously "sleep their last sleep" and are unable to fight.

❑ *Psalm 76:10.* Even the wrath of humanity will be turned into praise for God. The Hebrew text is difficult here, but the meaning seems to be that God will take the wrath that may be left and wear it like a shirt. (See the footnote in the NIV.)

❑ *Psalm 76:12.* God thoroughly controls the princes and kings of the world, even though they think they are in control.

❑ *Psalm 84.* This seems to be a pilgrimage psalm, sung by persons journeying to Jerusalem to worship. God's dwelling place is described as being lovely, a place to long for.

❑ *Psalm 84:5-7.* Those on pilgrimage describe the journey. Though it is difficult and dangerous, it is a joyous trip because at the end they will see "God in Zion."

❑ *Psalm 84:10-12.* Life in the Temple is far superior to life anywhere else.

❑ *Psalm 122.* This is another pilgrimage hymn. The worshipers have arrived in Jerusalem and admire the city.

❑ *Psalm 122:3-4.* The importance of Jerusalem for the psalm is its unifying force for the "tribes of the LORD." It symbolizes the unity that binds Israel together.

❑ *Psalm 122:9.* Prayer is offered for Jerusalem, because within its secure walls stands the "house of the LORD our God," the Temple. A safe Jerusalem ensures a safe Temple.

DIMENSION THREE:
WHAT DOES THE BIBLE MEAN TO ME?

Psalm 15
What Does the Lord Require of Me?

Who can worship God? How does one gain access to God? Psalm 15 and Psalm 24 affirm that God is far more interested in societal behavior than in appropriate worshiping forms on given holy days. You will note that neither of the entrance requirements given in the two psalms says or implies that bad theology separates one from God. What separates one from God is not being truthful, treachery, slander, bribery, and mistreatment of the poor. These are the behaviors that God is most interested in.

Right worship can be valuable, but God is much more concerned with right behavior. Jesus put it another way. "Not everyone who says to me, 'Lord, Lord,' will enter the kingdom of heaven, but only he who does the will of my Father who is in heaven" (Matthew 7:21). Again the emphasis is on right action, rather than right words. The prophets also spoke on this issue. (See Isaiah 1:11-17; Jeremiah 22:13-17; Amos 5:21-24; Micah 6:6-8.)

What is God's will for you in society? Is Amos correct when he emphasizes right action at the expense of appropriate worship? What does that mean for your life as a Christian? What should you do before worshiping the Lord? What is more important for you, right worship or right behavior?

Jerusalem: What's in It for Me?

A study of the songs of Zion demonstrates historically and theologically the meaning of Jerusalem for the people of Israel. Jerusalem is, of course, a definite geographic place. The city is located in the hill country of Judah in the southern region of Israel. It was captured by David from the Jebusites sometime before the year 1000 B.C. It became the city of David, his royal capital of a United Israel, and stood intact until the destruction by the Babylonians in 587 B.C. These historic facts of Jerusalem tell us only a very small part of the meaning of the place for generations of Israelites, even down to our own time.

Jerusalem is uniquely God's city. It is the place where God has caused the divine name to dwell. Pilgrims go up to Jerusalem knowing that the spot is holy. It was made so by the Temple, but more by God who has uniquely consecrated that Temple. God has literally made Jerusalem the center of the earth. From Jerusalem, a river streams to water God's land. There, the quarrels and hatreds of nations will cease when God destroys the weapons of war.

In Psalm 46:9 we can see that Jerusalem has become a symbol, the manifestation of God's coming kingdom on the earth. When Isaiah claims that many people shall come to Zion, to learn war no more (see Isaiah 2:1-4), he reiterates this same meaning. Jerusalem becomes for the Israelite psalmist the place of peace. Jerusalem is the center of God's coming kingdom. It is the symbol of justice, love, and peace in a world sorely in need of all of these.

Our world needs such a symbol, a visible sight of God's coming reign and God's active will. My journeys to Jerusalem have not provided me with much proof of this symbol. Tension, spiked with barbed wire and gun emplacements, greets every contemporary visitor. But the city itself is not the real point. The symbol of God's peace is what counts. This is why even after the city was reinhabited by Jews, every Jewish Passover meal, in the very city itself, ends with the phrase, "Next year in Jerusalem!" Wrapped up in that phrase are the hopes, aspirations, and dreams of a weary people who need some assurance of God's will for peace and justice. Do you have such a symbol in your life? If so, what is it? What are the symbols that provide meaning for your life?

*O LORD, the king rejoices in your
strength. / How great is his joy in the victories you give!
(21:1).*

—— 4 ——
Royal Psalms

• • •

DIMENSION ONE:
WHAT DOES THE BIBLE SAY?

Answer these questions by reading Psalm 2

1. Who stands with the Lord against the kings of the earth?
   (2:2)

2. What will the Lord do for the "Anointed One"? (2:8-9)

3. What should all earthly rulers do? (2:11)

Answer these questions by reading Psalm 18

4. How does the psalmist describe his difficulty to God?
   (18:4-5)

5. How is God described in the psalm? (18:2, 8-15)

6. Who is speaking in the psalm? (18:50)

Answer these questions by reading Psalm 20

7. Who is the "you" of Psalm 20:1? (20:1, 6)

8. In whom should we trust? (20:7)

Answer these questions by reading Psalm 21

9. Why should the king trust in the Lord? (21:7)

10. Whose strength is exalted in the poem, God's or the king's? (21:13)

Answer these questions by reading Psalm 45

11. Who is the psalmist here? (45:1)

12. How is the king described in the psalm? (45:2, 5)

Answer these questions by reading Psalm 72

13. What is the chief role of the king in Israel? (72:2)

14. Why is it hoped that the king endure "as long as the sun"? (72:5, 12-14)

15. What is the result of a righteous king? (72:1, 16)

Answer these questions by reading Psalm 89

16. Why is God described as "greatly feared" and "awesome"? (89:7, 9-13)

17. Who anoints the kings of Israel? (89:20)

18. How long will David's throne last? (89:29)

Answer these questions by reading Psalm 110

19. What will God do for "my Lord"? (110:1)

20. Who is Melchizedek? (110:4)

DIMENSION TWO:
WHAT DOES THE BIBLE MEAN?

The psalms covered in this lesson are Psalms 2, 18, 20, 21, 45, 72, 89, 110, and 144. Psalm 101 is also a royal psalm, but is not examined here. These royal psalms are focused on the subject of the king of Israel. In some of them we can detect specific occasions when the psalm may have been used, such as the king's wedding (Psalm 45) or the king's coronation (Psalms 2 and 110). In these psalms the king is depicted in a very positive light. You should remember, however, that the Bible is fully aware of the danger of kings who become drunk with power and forget their primary responsibility of service. The story of the rise of kingship in Israel is found in the Book of First Samuel. Both positive and negative views of kingship are expressed there. Samuel was reluctant to have a king. The royal psalms celebrate the king at his best, as we shall see.

❑ *Psalm 2:1-3.* This may very well be a coronation psalm. The nations of the world are described as plotting against God and against God's "Anointed One." This word in Hebrew is the word *messiah. Messiah* was originally a title for the anointed leader of Israel. After the end of the monarchy in Israel (after 587 B.C.), the title came to mean the ideal future king, who would restore the fortunes of Israel.

❑ *Psalm 2:4-9.* The king, in the ceremony of coronation, proclaims the gift of universal rule, granted by God. God has established the king on Zion, God's holy hill. In verse 7 we read that the king was thought to have been adopted as God's son when he was crowned (see 2 Samuel 7:14 and another royal psalm, 89:26-27, for a similar idea). Paul quotes verse 7 in a sermon at Antioch of Pisidia in Acts 13:33. Paul uses the passage as the early church in general did. The early church thought the psalm referred to Jesus, the Son of God.

The king has only to ask God, and God will give him the nations for his inheritance and all the ends of the earth for his possession. Coronation language for all kings the world over is grandiose and universal in tone.

❑ *Psalm 2:10-11.* All other earthly kings are urged to serve God and by implication to serve God's king in Jerusalem.

❑ *Psalm 18.* This psalm also appears in the Bible as 2 Samuel 22. Apparently some editors of the Old Testament inserted poems into narratives for artistic effect. This psalm was credited to David, as the heading makes clear and the Samuel version also indicates.

❑ *Psalm 18:4-5.* This psalm describes in lurid language the profound difficulty the psalmist is having. The language of these two verses is very typical of thanksgiving psalms and also of lament psalms. The imagery is certainly metaphorical. The mortal fears of the psalmist are described by the phrases *cords of death, torrents of destruction,* and *cords of the grave.* The more literal view of the psalmist's troubles is in verses 37-45. The real problem is one of military enemies.

❑ *Psalm 18:8-15.* That this psalm is quite old is made clear by the imagery used to describe God. If such language were used outside the Bible, we could only think of a great, flying dragon! The cherub being described is not one of those chubby-cheeked babies of Renaissance paintings. This is a fearsome creature. (See Genesis 3:24 for a description of the creature that guards the way to the tree of life.) This ancient language is designed to heighten the impact of the portrait. These dragon-like images were familiar to the Hebrews and thus could provide a vivid picture of the great God.

❑ *Psalm 18:50.* The subject of the psalm is the king and more specifically the Davidic king. God has uniquely chosen this king to do great deeds on God's behalf.

❑ *Psalm 20.* This psalm sounds like a prayer written before a battle, offered to the king for support and to be offered to God. The "you" of verse 1 is the king being buoyed up by the prayer.

❑ *Psalm 20:5-6.* The first half of the poem ends with the petition that "the LORD grant all your requests." The second half begins "Now I know that the LORD saves his anointed." Something has obviously taken place between verses 5 and 6. If we are dealing with a worship service here, we can assume that an oracle of victory has been offered by a priest or prophet, making the certainty of verse 6 possible. Other psalms seem to assume some otherwise unnamed liturgical event that moves the poem from one mood to another. (See, for example Psalms 6:9-10 and 28:5-6.) Exactly what occurred in between the mood shifts we can probably never know.

❑ *Psalm 20:7.* The nations are fond of trusting in their military prowess, chariots, and horses. But Israel trusts in the name of God who stands above any military force.

❑ *Psalm 21.* The king trusts God because of God's *hesed,* or "unfailing love." The word is usually used in contexts that describe the material liability of those who are relatives, friends, master and servant, or belonging to one another in any other way. God's *hesed* is primary in the divine-human relationship. The king can trust God, because God is known by eternal unfailing love.

❑ *Psalm 21:13.* The psalm ends in a very pointed way. Verses 8-12 describe how the king can and will do mighty deeds of many kinds. But no worshiper should make any mistake concerning the source of the king's victories. The king's power may be worthy of respect, but it is not worthy of human praise. Only God is worthy of praise.

❑ *Psalm 45.* This is quite obviously a wedding song for a royal marriage between "the most excellent of men" (verse 2) and a princess in "embroidered garments" (verses 13-14).

❑ *Psalm 45:1.* The author of the psalm is a court poet. Such a poet is some sort of professional author, who writes speedily like a scribe.

❑ *Psalm 45:2-9.* The king is described in the traditional language of such odes. He is beautiful, dressed in the finest of clothes, and smelling as fragrant as the finest of spices (verse 8). However, the poet intersperses these physical descriptions with the concerns that are always prominent in any talk of the king. He defends right and truth (verse 4); he loves righteousness and hates wickedness. The poet is not blinded by the majesty of the king so as to forget the king's function as defender of the truth.

❑ *Psalm 45:10-12.* The prospective queen is urged to forget her own ancestry (presumably she is a foreigner). She is advised to follow her lord, the king.

❑ *Psalm 45:16-17.* The king is promised sons by the poet and literary immortality through the poem.

❏ *Psalm 72:2-4, 12-14.* The chief function of the king in Israel is emphasized in this psalm. He is to defend the cause of the poor and needy and help those who have no helper. With these words the psalmist is united to the cause of the prophet. What the people need most from the king is for him to set the conditions so that "in his days the righteous will flourish; / prosperity will abound till the moon is no more" (verse 7). Leaders are to be judged on these bases rather than on power, beauty, or cleverness.

❏ *Psalm 72:16.* When the king is truly righteous, not only will the land be full of waving grain, but the cities themselves will be full of people.

❏ *Psalm 89.* This poem, like Psalm 18, is a lengthy prayer from the king for deliverance from his enemies. The king extols the power of God and then draws on that power for help.

❏ *Psalm 89:9-14.* Elements of an ancient creation hymn are used by the psalmist to describe God as just and terrible.

❏ *Psalm 89:20.* The poet affirms that God anoints kings and provides whatever power the king may have.

❏ *Psalm 89:27-29.* The psalmist reiterates the adoption formula of the king, as told by God. The Israelite king is God's "first-born." God's *hesed* (unfailing love) shall never be withdrawn from the king.

❏ *Psalm 89:46-51.* The psalm closes with a pitiful cry of the king who feels rejected and cast off by God.

❏ *Psalm 89:52.* This verse is not the end of Psalm 89. It is a doxology closing Book Three of the Psalter. (For a similar verse, see Psalm 41:13, a line that closes Book One of the Psalter.)

❏ *Psalm 110.* We should be careful not to force too much into the details of this psalm. The text of the Hebrew is unusually difficult. That means that the transmission of the text over the centuries has not been good. In spite of these difficulties in the text, this particular psalm has played a large role in early Christian reflection concerning the person of Jesus.

❏ *Psalm 110:1.* The "my Lord" of verse 1 is certainly the king of Israel.

❏ *Psalm 110:4.* The mysterious Melchizedek is mentioned only one other time in the Old Testament (see Genesis 14:18). The thought seems to be that like the ancient Melchizedek, who was the priest-king of Salem, the new king will have a priestly role to play. Because the name *Melchizedek* means "king of righteousness," or "my king is righteous," being like Melchizedek is particularly important for the Israelite king. As we have seen, the king is specially charged with the responsibility of maintaining righteousness for his people.

DIMENSION THREE: WHAT DOES THE BIBLE MEAN TO ME?

The Concept of the Messiah

The idea of a messiah, or "anointed one," is a *very* complex one. Our psalms give us only the beginning point where the king is called the messiah, the Anointed One of God. In fact, of the nearly forty uses of the noun *anointed* (meaning "messiah"), twenty-nine describe a king of Israel or Judah. Eight usages are for priests who later took on some of the roles earlier assigned to the kings. Once Cyrus, the Persian, is called messiah ("his anointed," Isaiah 45:1) in a shocking statement. In Psalm 105:15, the patriarchs are given the title. But, as you can see, the word *messiah* was almost exclusively a royal word.

When the kingship of Israel ended after the destruction of Jerusalem in 587 B.C., the title was removed from some physical king who no longer existed. It was then transferred to an ideal king. This ideal king would do all the things the psalms describe in a restored world where God's kingdom of peace and righteousness was evident. Thus it should not be surprising that the royal psalms were interpreted in later times as thoroughly messianic. (For example, Psalm 2 is quoted in Acts 4:25; 13:33; Hebrews 1:5; 5:5.)

The problem for later Judaism, as it divided itself from the early Christian church, was just *how* the messiah would perform the great work of the new king. A messiah who suffers and dies as a substitute for all persons, as one finds in the New Testament, is unknown to Judaism. Obviously, elements of such a view exist in the Old Testament (see Isaiah 53). However, the Christian view of the suffering and dying messiah is completely different from that of Judaism. This fact should help us see two important things. (1) Judaism is a different religion than Christianity. (2) The Jews of the first century could hardly have readily accepted a suffering, dying messiah.

Do these facts about the messianic views of the Bible change your ideas of the relationship between Christians and Jews? Why or why not? What is your view of Judaism as a religion?

The Great "I AM"

Psalm 18 might make one question who—or what—God is. God is called a rock, a fortress, a deliverer, a shield, and a stronghold. Verse 8 pictures smoke coming from God's nose and fire from his mouth. None of these descriptions is meant to picture God as a stone, or building, or dragon. They are metaphors intended to help us understand some of God's attributes. Language we use to describe God is an important issue for Christians.

I once heard the pastor of a congregation in which most of the members had hearing impairments tell a small boy with a hearing impairment that not only did God understand sign language; more than that, he said, God is hearing impaired. He said that God is hearing impaired because he wants that boy to know that God knows his problem and has real compassion for him.

Of course God is not really hearing impaired, but because God created each us us he is fully attuned to our needs. As God once became a baby, he is able and willing to come to us in our own form. It is perfectly acceptable to envision God meeting our individual personal needs by being with us in hearing impairment if that is what we need. Or supplying the guidance and nurturing of a father or mother as we have those needs.

When Moses asked God for his name, God replied that he is "I AM" (Exodus 3:13-14). No names we can call God will ever be sufficient because God cannot be contained by a name. When asked who he is, God replied not with a name, but a verb. Language about God should always be carefully used so that it is invitational. Every person in every set of circumstances should feel welcomed by the Christian community.

*Shout with joy to God, all the earth! / Sing
the glory of his name; / make his praise glorious! (66:1-2).*

— 5 —
Communal Thanksgiving Psalms

• • •

DIMENSION ONE:
WHAT DOES THE BIBLE SAY?

Answer these questions by reading Psalm 65

1. Where is God to be praised? (65:1, 4)

2. Why is praise due to God? (65:2, 5-8)

3. What do the streams of God provide? (65:9)

Answer these questions by reading Psalm 66

4. Who should shout with joy to God? (66:1)

5. What has God done that is worthy of praise? (66:5-7)

6. What does the worshiper do in response to God? (66:13-15)

Answer these questions by reading Psalm 67

7. Why will God be gracious to those who pray? (67:2)

8. How does God deal with the world? (67:4)

9. How can we know that God is with us? (67:6)

Answer these questions by reading Psalm 75

10. What do the worshipers say at the beginning of the psalm? (75:1)

11. In whom is God most interested? (75:4)

Answer these questions by reading Psalm 100

12. How should God be worshiped? (100:2)

13. Why should we praise the Lord as our God? (100:3)

14. Why is the Lord good? (100:5)

Answer these questions by reading Psalm 105

15. What is the key word in this psalm? (105:7-11)

16. What story is told in this psalm? (105:12-41)

17. What should be the people's response to God's great deeds? (105:45)

Answer these questions by reading Psalm 106

18. How is this story of God's great deeds different from that of Psalm 105? (106:6-7)

19. How does God respond to the continual sin of Israel? (106:44-46)

20. What should we do when we are saved by God? (106:47)

Answer these questions by reading Psalm 136

21. What is the refrain of the psalm? (136:1, 2, and so on)

22. Which deeds of God are emphasized here? (136:10-15)

23. Whom is God finally interested in? (136:25)

DIMENSION TWO:
WHAT DOES THE BIBLE MEAN?

The psalms covered in this lesson are Psalms 65, 66, 67, 75, 100, 105, 106, and 136. Psalms 107 and 124 are also thanksgiving psalms, but are not examined here. These communal thanksgiving psalms are exactly what their title suggests. They are hymns to God, thanking God for great past and present deeds. They are sung by groups, rather than by individuals. They generally begin with a call to all nations and all nature to praise God. Next comes a recital of the great deeds of history and nature for which God is worthy of praise. They end with a celebration of a present state of glorious blessings that God has given.

❏ *Psalm 65:1-4.* The literal reading of the first line is, "To you is due praise, God on Zion." In other words, the psalmist wants to emphasize the object of the praising words. Beginning the poem with a pronoun reference to God is unusual Hebrew word order. Note that God's unique place of praise is Zion, Jerusalem's holy hill. In verse 2, the universal praise of God is commanded in the phrase "to you all men will come."

❏ *Psalm 65:5-8.* The great deeds of God are now recounted. In this psalm the deeds are God's acts of physical creation. The reference in verse 7 to the stilling of the seas hints at the old

COMMUNAL THANKSGIVING PSALMS **41**

creation mythology of the combat between the gods and the waters to hammer out the world. God's victory over the creation, both physical and human, is complete.

❏ *Psalm 65:9-13.* The abundance of the land is now celebrated by the psalmist as a direct and delightful gift of God. God's gift of water refreshes the earth and provides for the bounty of the land. Note the mention again of the wonderful "streams of God" in verse 9. (See the discussion on Psalm 46:4 in Lesson 3.) This psalm probably had a close connection to the agricultural festival that celebrated and anticipated the return of the rains. Psalm 65 follows the literary pattern of the communal thanksgiving psalm perfectly.

❏ *Psalm 66:3.* The translation in the Revised Standard Version, "How terrible are their deeds!" is not wrong, but it is unfortunate. The word *terrible* is usually translated "fear," particularly in the King James Version. The preferable English word is *awe*. Awe is a mixed feeling of reverence, fear, and wonder. The words *awe* and *awesome* are closer in meaning to the original Hebrew word. *Awe* is generally used in both the New Revised Standard Version and the New International Version (NIV).

❏ *Psalm 66:5-7.* The awesome deeds of God this time are from Israel's history. Verse 6 refers to the two major water crossings of Israel's past, the Red Sea (or Sea of Reeds; Exodus 14) and the Jordan River (Joshua 3). "Come, let us rejoice in him," the psalmist goes on to say; but God's work hardly ended with those two acts of power. God now "rules forever by his power." For all this God is worthy of thanks and praise.

❏ *Psalm 66:10-12.* God tested the Israelites, and they survived, says the psalmist.

❏ *Psalm 66:13-15.* In response to God's actions, the worshiper vows to make an appropriate sacrifice of burnt offerings and will tell all what God has done (verse 16).

❏ *Psalm 67.* Once again this psalm demonstrates the threefold pattern of the communal thanksgiving psalm. Verse 3 is the call for all people to praise God. Verse 4 suggests the reason for the praise; God judges with justice and guides the nations. Verses 6-7 record the great blessings given by God, now demonstrated by a fruitful earth.

42

❑ *Psalm 67:1.* Here we find an echo of the very famous benedictory prayer from Numbers 6:24-26.

❑ *Psalm 67:2.* The psalmist asks for God's gracious favor to shower upon the people for a particular reason. Without God's grace as the first act, God's way and saving power cannot be learned and known on earth. In other words, before you and I can proclaim God's praise, we must have received and accepted from God the grace only God can provide.

❑ *Psalm 67:4.* The word translated "justly" comes from a verb that means to go straight as opposed to crooked. God's judging of the world is evenhanded, absolutely fair, not deviating from the correct and proper.

❑ *Psalm 67:7.* Again the translation "fear" should rather be "awe." "All the ends of the earth will be in awe of him."

❑ *Psalm 75:1.* This psalm is a liturgy of thanksgiving in the Temple. The assembled worshipers offer their thanks to God, a thanks based on God's "wonderful deeds."

❑ *Psalm 75:2-8.* At this point in the service, either a priest or a Temple prophet proclaims a divine oracle, prophesying judgment for the wicked. Verse 2 repeats the word of Psalm 67:4. God judges "uprightly," with straightness. In verse 3, we learn of God's power—in the midst of an earthquake it is God who brings the calm. Without the power of God, the tottering of the earth would continue until its complete destruction.

Using the horn as a symbol of power and strength, the proclamation warns the boastful and the wicked not to exalt themselves. As verses 6-7 indicate, exaltation or defeat do not come from any place in the world. They come only from God, who lifts up one while putting down another. Verse 8 provides a famous image of the foaming cup of the wine of wrath that all wicked persons will be forced to drink. This wine is a symbol of their final defeat by God. (See Isaiah 51:22-23; Jeremiah 25:15; 49:12 for a similar image.) Jesus' comment in the garden of Gethsemane about the "cup" that he hopes can pass from him is possibly a reference to this tradition (see Luke 22:42).

❑ *Psalm 75:9-10.* The psalm closes with an individual, perhaps the king, praising God (verse 9). God has cut off the horns of the wicked and has exalted the horns of the righteous.

COMMUNAL THANKSGIVING PSALMS

❏ *Psalm 100.* Again, the pattern is clear. "All the earth" is to "shout for joy" to God and to serve God joyfully (verse 1). We praise God because God made us to be the people of God, the very sheep of God's pasture (verse 3). The present state of blessing is indicated in spiritual rather than material ways (verse 5).

❏ *Psalm 100:3.* An interesting problem is in the text here. You probably know the middle line of verse 3 as "It is he that has made us, and not we ourselves." The present Hebrew text literally reads that way. However, some very early comments on that text indicate that many read the text as the NIV has it, "It is he who made us, and we are his." This reading involves a very small change in the text and could very well be correct.

❏ *Psalm 105.* The psalm begins with the universal call to praise God for God's wonderful deeds.

❏ *Psalm 105:7-11.* This psalm might very well be named the psalm of God's covenant, the key term used in describing God's past work with the people.

❏ *Psalm 105:12-41.* The psalm provides a fascinating history of Israel's past, embroidered with little details that are not all present in the original stories. For example, the psalmist describes how Joseph's brothers sold him into slavery with these words in verse 18: "They bruised his feet with shackles, / his neck was put in irons." Nothing like this occurs in the Genesis 37–38 account. The psalmist clearly uses the ancient tale to instruct the people about how God was able to bring victory when no hope seemed possible.

❏ *Psalm 105:45.* The psalm ends by suggesting that God has done all these great deeds in order that Israel might "keep [God's] precepts and observe his laws." In their keeping one finds the blessing of God presently manifested.

❏ *Psalm 106.* This psalm provides an interesting complement to Psalm 105. In that psalm the power of God in Israel's history was praised. But the sin of Israel and God's overcoming of that sin are highlighted in Psalm 106. One gets in these two psalms two very different views of the sacred history of Israel.

❏ *Psalm 106:6-43.* Here is the long, sordid tale of Israel's sin throughout its history, coupled with God's incredible will to forgive and to save.

44   PSALMS

❏ *Psalm 106:44-45.* No matter how often Israel proved rebellious, because of God's steadfast love God paid attention to their cries of distress and relented.

❏ *Psalm 106:47.* This verse indicates that at least in this form the psalm was written after the Babylonian Exile (after 587 B.C.). The people of Israel beg God to gather them again to their lost land in order that they might praise God's name.

❏ *Psalm 106:48.* This verse is not part of the original psalm. It closes Book Four of the Book of Psalms.

❏ *Psalm 136.* Psalm 136 is almost certainly a responsive reading with its repetitions of "His love endures forever." Within the psalm we find a brief history of the complete actions of God with Israel, from the creation of the world (verses 5-9), to the Exodus from Egypt (verses 10-15), to the gift of the Promised Land (verses 21-22). All these actions are results of God's eternal, unfailing love.

DIMENSION THREE:
WHAT DOES THE BIBLE MEAN TO ME?

God's Work in History

The communal thanksgiving psalms all emphasize God's actions within the history of Israel. Four chief events are celebrated. They are Creation, the Exodus, the wandering in the desert, and the gift of the land. In each of these actions, it is important for us to realize that the major concern of the psalmists was not to prove the precise historical details of these events. Rather, they wanted to celebrate the fact that God was carrying forward the promise given to Israel.

The psalms are not trying to present an exact history of the world, but to affirm that God had a hand in it. For example, Psalm 66:6 affirms that during the Exodus God "turned the sea into dry land," not caring how or where or when. Psalm 106:9-11 claims the same: the sea dried up, and the waters covered their adversaries. Psalm 136:13-15 says that God "cut the Reed Sea into pieces, and brought Israel into its midst, but shook Pharaoh and his strength into the Reed Sea" (my translation). Again the simple outlines are there without details needed or noted. What counts for the psalmists is their constant affirmation that God has acted in the life of Israel. Because God has acted then, we can expect and hope that God will act for us. In effect, the psalms of Israel are a long attempt to say one very simple thing: "You did it before, God; now do it again for me!"

This idea can have great importance for us. We affirm that God has acted in our history by raising Jesus from the dead. If you were to ask other Christians how they understand that event in history, you would probably not receive a unanimous answer. Some would believe that God did actually at one time and in one place raise Jesus from the dead. Some might see the event in a more symbolic way. They may feel that the death of Jesus was not the final word of God. God determined that life, through suffering service, was the word that needed to be heard. Perhaps you have other suggestions to make here.

Whatever we believe about the event of God's victory through Jesus Christ, we are called to celebrate not only that victory. If we are not raised by God in our lives, then we cannot understand or have not understood God's act in Jesus of Nazareth. I had a wonderful member of the church I was serving in Louisiana tell me that she never understood resurrection until her husband died. What she meant was that if God had not raised her from her death-like grief and pain she might as well have been dead. Her resurrection by God helped her to praise God as a God of resurrection.

Thus, with the psalmists we need to celebrate God's past actions, in whatever way we understand those actions. But also we must affirm that God is acting now for us, and praise God for that as well. If I cannot see God's actions today, then any past actions of God can have no meaning for me at all.

How do you understand God's actions in the history of the biblical people? Are these actions important for you? How?

When I felt secure, I said, /
"I will never be shaken" (30:6).

—— 6 ——

Individual Thanksgiving Psalms

● ● ●

DIMENSION ONE:
WHAT DOES THE BIBLE SAY?

Answer these questions by reading Psalm 30

1. Why does the psalmist exalt the Lord? (30:1-2)

2. Who is to sing praises to the Lord? (30:4)

3. How long does God's anger last? (30:5)

Answer these questions by reading Psalm 32

4. What happened when the psalmist kept silent? (32:3)

5. Who should offer prayer to God? (32:6)

6. Why shouldn't we be like the horse and the mule? (32:8-9)

Answer these questions by reading Psalm 34

7. When will the psalmist extol the Lord? (34:1)

8. Whom does God especially see and hear? (34:15)

9. The Lord is close to whom? (34:18)

Answer these questions by reading Psalm 40

10. How many wonders has God done for us? (40:5)

11. What does God not desire? (40:6)

12. What is in the heart of the psalmist? (40:8)

Answer these questions by reading Psalm 41

13. What seems to be the problem of this psalmist? (41:3)

14. Who has turned against the psalmist? (41:5, 9)

15. How does the psalmist know that God is there? (41:11)

Answer these questions by reading Psalm 92

16. When should God be praised? (92:2)

17. What are the wicked compared to? (92:7)

18. What are the righteous compared to? (92:12)

Answer these questions by reading Psalm 116

19. Why does the psalmist love the Lord? (116:1)

20. Who causes "dismay" in the psalmist? (116:11)

21. What does the psalmist offer to God? (116:17)

22. Who should proclaim "His love endures forever"? (118:1-4)

23. For what is the psalmist thankful to God? (118:10)

24. What should we do in the day that God has made? (118:24)

DIMENSION TWO:
WHAT DOES THE BIBLE MEAN?

The psalms covered in this lesson are Psalms 30, 32, 34, 40, 41, 92, 116, and 118. Psalms 103, 111, and 138 are also thanksgiving psalms, but are not examined here. In the previous lesson we examined communal thanksgiving psalms. Here we look at individual thanksgiving psalms.

The only real difference in communal thanksgiving psalms and individual thanksgiving psalms is that the individual, who apparently speaks in these poems, gives them a far more personal tone. Thus, the element of lament is more prominent in these psalms than in the similar communal thanksgiving psalms. You should note this personal element of lament as you read the psalms for the lesson.

❏ *Psalm 30.* This psalm was sung "for the dedication of the temple." This does not mean necessarily the original Temple's dedication in the tenth century B.C. It may mean the rededication of the Temple by the Maccabees in 164 B.C. This then is an example of a psalm originally composed for individual use that was later used in a Temple service by the worshipers.

❑ *Psalm 30:3.* God's salvation of the individual is given in extreme images of life and death. The word translated as "me" in the NIV and as "soul" in the NRSV means one's very life, body, and spirit. The word *pit* is a quite specific term, often used to refer to a water cistern, a rock-lined hole in the ground used for collecting precious rain water. It becomes a metaphor for the place of the dead in Ezekiel and in the Psalms.

❑ *Psalm 30:4.* The word translated "saints" is the word *hasid* in Hebrew, a noun form related to the word *hesed*, or unfailing love. These are persons who are especially devoted to God and usually devout. Later in Jewish history the *hasidim* were devout Jewish scholars and mystics.

❑ *Psalm 30:6-7.* The psalmist had become self-satisfied, feeling perfectly safe and secure. Then God's face was hidden and the psalmist was "dismayed."

❑ *Psalm 30:8-10.* The psalmist, whose pride is now broken, turns to God in lament, asks God to be a helper, and asks God "will the dust praise you?" This implies that the dead do not praise God (see Psalm 6:5 and Isaiah 38:18).

❑ *Psalm 30:12.* In response to God's help the psalmist vows praise and thanks forever.

❑ *Psalm 32:3.* The psalmist blames the disease on the fact that he did not admit to a hidden fault or transgression. When the bad deed or idea was confessed, God's response was to bring healing. Disease was commonly considered punishment for sin.

❑ *Psalm 32:6.* "Everyone who is godly" is called to offer prayer to God. The word *godly* here is the same word translated "saint" in Psalm 30:4.

❑ *Psalm 32:8-11.* This part of the psalm uses expressions one finds most often in the Book of Proverbs. Verse 8 describes God as the teacher while the suppliant and hearers are the students. God teaches, instructs, and counsels. Verse 9 uses two proverbially strong and stubborn creatures to warn the pupils against resistance to the teacher. The sharp distinction between the wicked and the righteous is drawn at the end of the psalm, again like the moral teaching of Proverbs. (See, for example, Proverbs 21:12, 26.)

INDIVIDUAL THANKSGIVING PSALMS

❏ *Psalm 34.* Like Psalms 9, 10, and 25 this psalm is an alphabetic acrostic. Each line begins with a successive Hebrew letter. This artificial construction lends itself to the apparent intent of the poem to teach that God always knows the sharp difference between the wicked and the righteous. In the end, the wicked perish and the righteous triumph. Note that eternal life is not mentioned. The division of wicked and righteous would have to be found in this life.

The title of the psalm gives a clue to its historical association, at least in the minds of the persons who collected the psalms. Just why this psalm should be attached to the incident of 1 Samuel 21:13-15, and why the name of the Philistine king Achish, found in Samuel, should have been changed here to Abimelech is impossible to determine.

❏ *Psalm 34:15.* God listens most carefully to the righteous. They speak no evil and "seek peace" (verses 13-14). Also, the righteous are identified with persons with broken hearts and crushed spirits (verse 18).

❏ *Psalm 40.* In this psalm, we clearly move from an older idea of sacrificial worship as a response to God to a more active concern with the doing of God's will in society. The emphasis is toward a more spiritualized cult. The singing of the psalm itself may begin to replace the older sacrificial system.

❏ *Psalm 40:4.* The word translated "proud" in the NIV is in reality the plural form of the word *Rahab*, a mythological creature. Apparently, the psalmist here warns us against turning toward Rahab or false gods.

❏ *Psalm 40:7.* For the idea of the "scroll," or roll book, where names and deeds are written, see Psalms 56:8 and 139:16.

❏ *Psalm 40:6-8.* These verses are quoted in the New Testament in Hebrews 10:5-7. If you read that passage, however, you will note some rather sharp differences. The author of Hebrews is apparently not quoting from the Hebrew text but from the Greek translation of the Old Testament made in the third century B.C.

❏ *Psalm 41.* Again we find a psalm of thanksgiving for the healing of disease. But this time the enemies of the psalmist, and even one of the dearest friends, seem to be implicated in the illness in some kind of magical way. God provides the healing, but the enemies aid the sickness.

❑ *Psalm 41:5-8.* These four verses describe a very ancient belief that enemies can affect the cause of an illness for evil intent. Note how the "speaking" of evil is emphasized here. The psalmist is being made ill by the magic speaking of enemies. Even the closest friend has "lifted up his heel against" him (the phrase is difficult to translate). Only God could have saved the worshiper from these evil magicians.

❑ *Psalm 41:13.* This is the closing doxology of Book One of the Psalms and not part of Psalm 41.

❑ *Psalm 92.* The title says this is a song to sing on the Sabbath. Later in the life of Judaism, the worshipers apparently hesitated to write many new songs for their emerging and diversifying cult. They just chose the old psalms to use for the different occasions in their worshiping lives. As a result of this tendency, Psalm 92 became a psalm to be sung on the Sabbath, rather than on any specific feast day.

❑ *Psalm 92:5-9.* God's words are great. God's thoughts are deep. "The senseless man" (verse 6), the most stupid of people, cannot understand that though the wicked sprout like grass, they are doomed. The psalm does not really address the question of why the wicked prosper. It merely attacks those who disagree.

❑ *Psalm 92:12-14.* The wicked "spring up like grass," short-rooted and short-lived (verse 7). But the righteous flourish like deep-rooted and long-lived palm trees or cedar trees. Moreover, they are planted in the very house of God, where they are "fresh and green" (verse 14).

❑ *Psalm 116:3.* The psalmist's anguish (disease) is described in this lament in terms of imminent death—the "cords of death" and the "anguish of the grave."

❑ *Psalm 116:10-11.* Even when the psalmist feels most put upon, most attacked, he still keeps faith (literally stands firm). The psalmist was still capable of seeing that human beings were not the place to turn for ultimate help.

❑ *Psalm 116:15.* One might better get the intent of this verse by reading the phrase, "It is difficult for God when holy ones (devoted ones, saints) die." This reading would indicate the personal anguish of God at the death of one of these most devoted ones. However, one might also read, "It is rare." In other words, the death of one of these does not occur very often. The phrase is not an easy one to be certain about.

❏ **Psalm 116:17.** Here the psalmist promises a sacrifice to God because of God's action on the psalmist's behalf. As opposed to Psalm 40:6-8, where sacrifice is not given, the psalmist here vows to give it.

❏ **Psalm 118.** In many ways, this psalm is the most clearly liturgical psalm we have thus far examined. Beginning in verse 19, we can readily see that the psalm depicts a festal procession. The gates of the sanctuary are asked to be opened. They have been opened, and the worshiper speaks from within the sanctuary (verse 26). Verse 27 apparently describes a procession by torchlight, leading right up to the sacred altar covered with branches.

❏ **Psalm 118:3.** The association of the psalm with the Temple is made more clear by the mention of the "house of Aaron," the traditional priestly family of Israel.

❏ **Psalm 118:22-23.** The New Testament uses these words as a reference to the rejection and exaltation of Jesus. (See Matthew 21:42; Acts 4:11; 1 Peter 2:7.) In the context of the psalm the words apparently refer to the worshiper who while first rejected is now highly exalted by God.

DIMENSION THREE:
WHAT DOES THE BIBLE MEAN TO ME?

Psalm 32:3—Is There Punishment for Sin?

Psalm 32 suggests very clearly that unconfessed sin leads to disease of the body (Psalm 32:3). Is evil a punishment for sin? Does God bring bad things to those who most richly deserve them? Several of this group of psalms, as we have seen, indicate clearly that God rewards the righteous and dooms the wicked. But a moment's thought makes such a position really quite appalling. Do tornadoes only strike wicked towns? Does cancer only attack evil persons? The answer to both those questions is an emphatic, "No."

God is not all crystal clear. The world is no logical theorem to be proved and mastered. Life is a mystery. So, though the psalmist may say on occasion that only "senseless" people do not believe that God always rewards the righteous (see Psalm 92:6), reality will not bear such a view. How have you answered this vexing question for your own faith? What examples can you cite from the Bible where the righteous are punished? Share these examples with the class.

No Immortality in the Psalms

No clear reference to eternal life is in the psalms. When the psalmists speak of Sheol, they refer to a shadowy place where everybody goes at death. But this place is not any sort of reward or punishment for deeds in life. Sheol is merely the home of the dead. Even the last line of Psalm 23, "I will dwell in the house of the LORD forever," is not a reference to eternal life. Rather, it is a statement that the Temple will be a place where the psalmist will return "as long as he lives" (a more accurate reading of the Hebrew text).

No direct talk of eternal life is in evidence. But the psalmist's trust in the power, might, and love of God forms the foundation for a belief that nothing can separate us from God's love. The claim that God can recover persons from the jaws of Sheol (the grave) (Psalms 30:2-3; 56:13) and that God is to be found in every part of the creation, even Sheol (139:8), eventually leads to a belief in immortality. The lofty ethical views of the Hebrews were forged under a this-worldly horizon completely. No afterlife was developed to affect their reflection on the basic ways humans were to live with and relate to one another.

What role does a belief in immortality play in your understanding of how you are to live with your fellow human beings? Without such a belief, could you have a faith? If so, how would it be different from the one you possess?

My God, my God, why have
you forsaken me? (22:1).

7

Individual Laments

● ● ●

DIMENSION ONE:
WHAT DOES THE BIBLE SAY?

Answer these questions by reading Psalm 3

1. What are the psalmist's foes saying? (3:2)

2. What does the psalmist ask of God? (3:7)

3. How does God respond? (3:7)

Answer these questions by reading Psalm 5

4. When is the psalmist praying? (5:3)

5. Where does the psalmist want to go? (5:7)

6. How does the psalmist describe the enemies? (5:9)

Answer these questions by reading Psalm 6

7. What is the psalmist's condition? (6:2-3)

8. Can God be praised from the grave? (6:5)

9. What will happen to the psalmist's enemies? (6:10)

Answer these questions by reading Psalm 7

10. How does the psalmist proclaim innocence? (7:3-5)

11. What does the psalmist want God to do? (7:6, 8)

12. What does the psalmist vow to do? (7:17)

Answer these questions by reading Psalm 9

13. What has happened to the enemy? (9:6)

14. Who seeks the Lord? (9:9-10)

15. If God answers, what will the psalmist do? (9:14)

Answer these questions by reading Psalm 10

16. What are the first questions of the psalmist? (10:1)

17. What is the wicked person's chief statement? (10:4, 6)

18. What will God finally do? (10:17-18)

Answer these questions by reading Psalm 14

19. What does the fool say? (14:1)

20. Are there any good people? (14:3)

21. What will God do for Israel? (14:7)

Answer these questions by reading Psalm 22

22. Does God answer the psalmist? (22:2)

23. How does the psalmist describe the problem? (22:12-18)

24. Who will finally worship God? (22:27)

DIMENSION TWO:
WHAT DOES THE BIBLE MEAN?

The psalms covered in this lesson are Psalms 3, 5, 6, 7, 9, 10, 14, and 22. Psalms 4, 13, 17, and 25 are also individual laments, but are not examined here. We now begin the first of five lessons on the lament psalms. Fully sixty-five of the 150 psalms are categorized as lament psalms. Many of these psalms have a sharper tone than we are used to. They are bold and demanding of God. The religion of the lament psalm is bold and brassy, sometimes arrogant, often pleading and cajoling. As we will see, many, if not most of the psalms are more complaint than they are lament.

Lament psalms first feature an address to God. Then the psalmist makes an initial general request for help from God. This is followed by a very specific request for help, often tied to an expression of trust. Next comes the complaint, or why help is needed, and finally some sort of movement beyond request and complaint.

❏ *Psalm 3.* This psalm is connected in its title to a specific event in David's life. The story of David being driven out of Jerusalem by his son Absalom is found in 2 Samuel 15. The collectors of the psalms probably connected this psalm to David because it is a royal lament and asks God for help against multiple foes.

❏ *Psalm 3:1.* "O LORD" is the simple address of this lament. Connected to it is an initial, implied exclamation of despair ("how many are my foes!").

❏ *Psalm 3:2.* Many laments describe the enemies as saying "God will not deliver him." In this way the psalmist urges God to rise up in his behalf. God needs to come to defend God's honor!

❑ *Psalm 3:4.* Now appears the specific, direct request, "To the LORD I cry aloud."

❑ *Psalm 3:6.* The reason for the request, the lament, appears here. The reason is more indirect than it usually is. The psalmist is not afraid of "the tens of thousands drawn up against" him.

❑ *Psalm 3:7.* "Arise, O LORD" is another direct request.

❑ *Psalm 3:8.* Here is the movement beyond request and lament that takes the form of an affirmation and a prayer request ("May your blessing be on your people").

In lament psalms, the psalmist prays in anticipation of God's help. In the thanksgiving psalms, however, the psalmist is grateful for favors already bestowed.

❑ *Psalm 5.* This psalm is presented in a liturgical setting. The psalmist prepares a morning sacrifice for God and awaits the coming of God's word (verse 3).

❑ *Psalm 5:5.* The word translated "all who do wrong" means more than evil. There's evil in it, but also mystery and magic. These are no ordinary evildoers, but mysterious persons of power whom only God can defeat.

❑ *Psalm 5:7.* The psalmist vows to worship God in the Temple but knows that only God's "great mercy" will make that possible.

❑ *Psalm 5:9.* The enemies are described in the most horrible of ways.

❑ *Psalm 5:11.* In contrast to the foul mouths of the enemies, the psalmist asks God to allow persons who trust the Lord to "sing for joy" and "rejoice" in God.

❑ *Psalm 6:3.* The anguish of this lament calls forth a plaintive cry common in the lament psalms, "how long?" (See Psalms 74:10; 80:4; 90:13; 94:3.) These psalms ask about God's plan and suggest rashly that "enough is enough!"

❑ *Psalm 6:4-5.* Verse 4 sounds like a rather traditional request to God to save the life of the psalmist "because of your unfailing love." But then the psalmist gives the reason why God should save him (verse 5). The psalmist is saying, "If you do not hurry and save me, God, you will lose another worshiper because dead people can offer no praise. People don't remember God when they are dead." This is a bold psalmist indeed!

❏ *Psalm 6:8.* This phrase is also found in Psalm 5:5. The "all you who do evil" are performing their evil acts (perhaps a curse?), but God has heard.

❏ *Psalm 6:9-10.* Some assurance has apparently been given that God has heard the prayer of the sufferer. This may be another time when, in the service of worship, a word of assurance was given by a priest or prophet, but not recorded in the psalm.

❏ *Psalm 6:10.* Once the Lord accepts the prayer, all the enemies shall be shamed in a moment.

❏ *Psalm 7:1-2.* Several interesting features appear in this lament, though the introductory address and request are quite traditional for these psalms.

❏ *Psalm 7:3-5.* The lament itself, usually the very heart of these psalms, is replaced by an oath of innocence. As proof of innocence the psalmist utters an oath of innocence. If the psalmist has in any way lied or done any evil deeds, then he asks for the enemy to triumph. By doing this the psalmist hopes to coax God to intervene. Other places in the Old Testament employ similar oaths of innocence (see Job 31; Psalms 17:3-4; 26:4-6). These oaths may be rhetorical in nature, uttered by the worshiper in preparation to receive a word from God.

❏ *Psalm 7:8.* After swearing innocence, the psalmist asks to be judged by God, who can readily see the psalmist's integrity now.

❏ *Psalm 7:12-16.* These verses have textual problems. Verses 12-13 apparently mean that if God does not change God's mind about the wicked, then God will do all those things to the wicked person. Verse 14 is a parody of the birth process. Verse 15 describes how the wicked carefully dig pits and fall right into them. The wicked are not only dangerous; they are stupid and comical.

❏ *Psalm 7:17.* The psalmist, in anticipation of God's actions against the wicked, vows to thank God and to sing praises to God as well.

❏ *Psalm 9.* In reality, Psalms 9 and 10 are one psalm, now artificially divided. Together they form one acrostic poem. (See pages 51–52 and 16 for our discussion of Psalms 34 and

145.) This acrostic is slightly different in that every second verse begins with a successive letter of the Hebrew alphabet. This acrostic style is so artificial that a logical train of thought is hardly to be anticipated. Psalm 9 is in actuality a hymn. But it is an anticipatory hymn, awaiting the deliverance of God.

❑ *Psalm 9:13.* This description of trouble is an element of a lament.

❑ *Psalm 9:16.* The meaning of *Higgaion* is unknown, though it must be similar to *Selah.*

❑ *Psalm 10:1.* Now the proper lament begins with a charge to God, asking why God appears to be unavailable.

❑ *Psalm 10:4.* Appearing to be triumphant, the wicked person says, "There is no room for God." Later, a hapless victim of the wicked says more stupidly that God has forgotten and has not seen (verse 11).

❑ *Psalm 10:12-13.* The psalmist calls God to task. How can the wicked talk in such a blasphemous way?

❑ *Psalm 10:14-18.* The remainder of the psalm affirms that God will not forget orphans and victims.

❑ *Psalm 14.* This psalm is nearly identical with Psalm 53. Although this is a lament psalm, it has no address to God and has a more general air to it. The psalmist appears to view his troubles as typical of a basically evil generation.

❑ *Psalm 14:1.* The word *fool* is not a light word, but one that indicates a deeply corrupted moral character.

❑ *Psalm 14:2-4.* The grim fact for this psalmist is that there are no righteous persons to be found anywhere.

❑ *Psalm 14:7.* The psalmist hopes for the complete restoration of Zion, but God will have to perform the act. We can see how this psalm could have been used as a nationalistic one, hoping for the restoration of a lost land.

❑ *Psalm 22.* This psalm was made famous for Christians by Jesus' use of the first line while on the cross. (See the words of Jesus, Matthew 27:46 and Mark 15:34.) The psalm is a classic lament. It contains the address (verse 1a), the complaint (verses 1b-2), an expression of confidence in God designed to motivate God's intervention (verses 4-5), why God's help is needed (verses 12-18), a request (verses 19-21), and a vow of praise (verses 22-31).

❏ *Psalm 22:16-18.* Given the close connection of this psalm to the events surrounding the crucifixion of Jesus, verse 16 needs to be clear. To read verse 16 "they have pierced" is not to read the Hebrew. "They have bound my hands and feet" better fits the context of the company of wicked persons assailing the sufferer. Jerome, in his Latin translation known as the Vulgate, used "pierced" here and thus fixed the reading for thirteen centuries.

❏ *Psalm 22:21.* A difficult text confronts us here. (See the text note in the NIV.) Adding "you have heard me" makes sense of the sharp change from verse 21 to verse 22. God has answered, and so the sufferer will now praise the name of God (verse 22).

DIMENSION THREE:
WHAT DOES THE BIBLE MEAN TO ME?

Prayer to God

Once there was a town drunk who liked to go fishing. He once had many fishing buddies, but his drinking got so bad that they all refused to go with him except the local minister who felt he had the obligation to be with the poor man. One day, the two of them were out in the boat on a rather threatening, overcast day. Suddenly, a violent storm hit them before they could row back to land. As the drunk grew more and more fearful, he suddenly stood up in the boat and swore at God every foul word he could think of. He blamed God in the bluest of language for everything wrong with the world, from war to pestilence to famine to his own drinking.

After a time, the storm stilled and the drunk fell back into the bottom of the boat. He turned to the pastor and said, "Well, preacher, I bet you never heard God spoken to like that before!" "Oh, I've heard worse," said the cleric, "and I imagine so has God. And, you know, what you said was the beginning of prayer." The drunk had nothing to say to that!

The beginning of prayer? Curse words from a drunk? Prayer to God can only begin in honesty. The drunk's anguish was torn out of him by fear of the storm. He instinctively turned to the Source of power to pour out his heart in the harsh and crude way he knew. This was the beginning of prayer.

This story might help us understand some of the really shocking prayers of the lament psalms, "I am innocent; you had better save me, if you are really God," reads Psalm 17. "Dead people do not praise God, so if you want some praise, you better get here fast," says Psalm 6. "How long?" cries the same psalm. "I cry day and night, but I hear no answer," says Psalm 22. These are all honest cries of anguish and despair, for these psalmists know what you and I try to avoid. Until we have faced the real despair of our lives and our world, we can never know the hope that only God can bring. Real prayer must begin in absolute honesty, or it is not prayer at all.

How do you pray? Do you bring to God your deepest fears, your ardent dreams? Or do you pray only what is familiar to what is given to you by someone else?

*"Show me, O Lord, my life's end, . . . /
let me know how fleeting is my life" (39:4).*

—— 8 ——

Individual Laments

• • •

DIMENSION ONE:
WHAT DOES THE BIBLE SAY?

Answer these questions by reading Psalm 27

1. How is the Lord described in this psalm? (27:1)

2. What does this psalmist most desire? (27:4)

3. Who are the enemies of the psalmist? (27:10, 12)

Answer these questions by reading Psalm 28

4. What is God called? (28:1, 7, 9)

5. What will God do to the wicked? (28:5)

6. What are the two repeated words used to describe God? (31:2-3)

7. Why does the psalmist trust God? (31:15)

Answer these questions by reading Psalm 35

8. Who will pursue the wicked adversaries of the psalmist? (35:5-6)

9. How are the psalmist's enemies described? (35:11)

Answer these questions by reading Psalm 38

10. Who has brought on the illness of the psalmist? (38:1-2)

11. How do the friends respond to the illness? (38:11)

12. How does the psalmist attempt to gain God's help? (38:18)

Answer these questions by reading Psalm 39

13. What does the psalmist want to know? (39:4)

14. What is the psalmist's final request to God? (39:13)

Answer these questions by reading Psalm 42

15. How is the psalmist's desire for God described? (42:1)

16. What do the men say to the psalmist? (42:3)

17. What does the psalmist say to his own soul? (42:11)

Answer this question by reading Psalm 43

18. How does the psalmist describe these enemies? (43:1)

Answer these questions by reading Psalm 51

19. Against whom has the psalmist sinned? (51:4)

20. What does God require of the psalmist? (51:6)

INDIVIDUAL LAMENTS

21. What does the psalmist ask of God? (51:10)

22. What is an acceptable sacrifice to God? (51:17)

DIMENSION TWO:
WHAT DOES THE BIBLE MEAN?

The psalms covered in this lesson are 27, 28, 31, 35, 38, 39, 42, 43, and 51. Psalms 26, 36, 52, and 53 are also individual laments, but are not examined here.

❑ *Psalm 27.* This psalm has a rather different order of the elements of a lament. The vow of praise, usually at the end of laments, is here in the middle at verse 6, leaving the lament (verse 12) and the request (verse 14) for the end.

❑ *Psalm 27:3.* The words *army* and *besiege* are military in origin, a fact made certain by the use of the word *war* in the same verse. Even if war rages against the psalmist, no fear will be found, because God is the psalmist's "light," "salvation," and "stronghold."

❑ *Psalm 27:4.* Here the psalmist wants to go to God's house in order to "seek him in his temple." The verb *seek* is here a technical term and means to seek a word from God. In other words, the psalmist wants to find a definite word from God.

❑ *Psalm 27:5.* The word *dwelling* is God's booth. A booth was a kind of lean-to connected in Israel's worship with the desert experience before the people entered the Promised Land. God's "tabernacle" may bring to mind the Tent of Meeting, also a device of the desert, when God communicated to the people. "Rock" may be a reference to the rock of Sinai, where God spoke to Moses. The psalmist reminds the worshipers of earlier times when God was available to the people.

❑ *Psalm 27:13.* The Hebrew of this verse literally reads, "If I had not believed I would see Yahweh's goodness in the land of the living. . . ." The sentence has no end. Either the end was dropped or we cannot understand the grammar. The NIV follows the Greek translation of the Hebrew text.

❑ *Psalm 28:1.* This psalm has a more typical address, request, and lament at the beginning. The word *pit* has a basic meaning of "cistern" or "well," but here it is a synonym for Sheol, the place of the dead.

❑ *Psalm 28:8.* The term *anointed one* (*messiah*) probably refers to the king for whom God is a refuge.

❑ *Psalm 31:13.* These words are similar to the lament of Jeremiah found in Jeremiah 20:10. Nearly every book in the Bible has some psalm literature in it.

❑ *Psalm 31:15.* The statement, "My times are in your hand," summarizes for the psalmist the reason for trust. God is in control and is present even when all appearances speak otherwise.

❑ *Psalm 31:21-24.* Again we may have some evidence of an oracle that provided assurance that the psalmist had been heard. Verse 24 indicates that the psalmist has been heard and exhorts others to be strong. God will answer.

❑ *Psalm 35:1.* The word translated "contend" is a legal term that could be translated "go to court with." The prophets use this language to describe God as having a case against Israel, which is accused of injustice and idolatry. (See Hosea 4:1; 12:2; Micah 6:2.) Here in this psalm God is called to go to court against the enemies of the psalmist.

❑ *Psalm 35:1-6.* The psalmist seems deeply offended by the attacks of the enemies, and thus searches for vengeance. The word translated "angel" is in reality a very general term that means messenger. The word would not have meant our idea of angels in wings and robes. That idea of angels is a far later development.

❑ *Psalm 35:11.* The enemies are said to be "ruthless witnesses." Another translation might be "ministers of violence." The word *violence* is connected with the prophetic tradition of oppression and injustice. "Violence" brought on the Flood (Genesis 6:11, 13), and Jeremiah claims that Jerusalem's eventual destruction will be due to violence (Jeremiah 6:7). (See also Amos 6:3.) The psalmist's complaint is thus tied to the

INDIVIDUAL LAMENTS **69**

great complaints of the past. Only God can deal with this problem.

This psalm has more than one complaint section. Note that verses 1-10, 11-18, and 19-28 could all be treated as separate lament units. The cumulative effect of the three laments is greater than any one lament by itself.

❑ *Psalm 38.* This psalm is based on the ancient belief that illness was a punishment for sin, or the doctrine of strict retribution. The story of Job deals with this same ancient belief.

❑ *Psalm 38:1-2.* The psalmist knows that God's arrows and hand have caused the illness. Unlike Job, who refuses to admit any sin, this psalmist confesses.

❑ *Psalm 38:11.* The response of the psalmist's friends and companions is to stand far away. Even the relatives want nothing to do with the sick person. They all reason, apparently, that if sickness is in evidence, God's anger must be great against the sick one.

❑ *Psalm 39:1-3.* This psalm begins without an address to God. The psalmist was in some sort of great distress, but refused to complain about it for fear of admitting to the wicked that doubts about God's justice and goodness were appearing.

❑ *Psalm 39:4-6.* The psalmist can keep silent no longer. But instead of chiding the enemies, the psalmist chides God for God's refusal to tell the psalmist just how brief life will be. The word *breath* of verse 5 is the same word translated in the first chapter of Ecclesiastes as *vanity.* It means mist or wind. The word suggests something insubstantial, reached for but slipping through the fingers.

❑ *Psalm 39:7-11.* Now the psalmist calls on God to deliver. But verse 10 goes right back to a request to God to stop attacking the psalmist. Verse 11 accuses God of going too far to punish sin. God consumes a person's glory like a moth, the most insubstantial of creatures.

❑ *Psalm 39:13.* The last word from the psalmist is a demand for God to get away long enough for the psalmist to know a little joy "before I depart and am no more." This shocking request is again similar to Job's (see Job 7:16 and 10:20-22).

❑ *Psalms 42–43.* These two psalms together form one song. There are three stanzas in the psalm, clearly marked off by the identical refrains of 42:5; 42:11; 43:5. Thus, 42:1-4 is stanza one, 42:6-10 is stanza two, and 43:1-4 is stanza three. This psalm was apparently composed by a person who was prevented from going on pilgrimage to Jerusalem.

❑ *Psalm 42:1-4.* With the vivid and unforgettable image of verse 1, the psalmist's deep desire to go to Jerusalem to the Temple is pictured. The psalmist remembers the previous journeys where he headed the faithful pilgrims right to the "house of God" (verse 4).

❑ *Psalm 42:5.* The refrain is designed to bring up the sagging faith of the psalmist. Most of the lament psalms provide us with examples of faith and hope when they are least expected.

❑ *Psalm 42:6.* The psalmist lives in the north of Israel near Mount Hermon and the origins of the Jordan.

❑ *Psalm 43:2-3.* In the third stanza of the song, the psalmist resolves to quit mourning and go to Jerusalem led by God's light and truth. Psalms 42 and 43 are wonderful affirmations of faith in the midst of hardship.

❑ *Psalm 51.* This psalm might be entitled a penitential lament. Its chief concern is with the admission of sin. Indeed, it is the clearest such psalm in the Book of Psalms. This helps to explain why the psalm became connected with the story of David's affair with Bathsheba. When David is confronted by Nathan, he admits his sins. This psalm became part of the remembrance of David's willingness to repent.

❑ *Psalm 51:1-4.* The psalmist admits sinning and implies that all evil deeds are ultimately against God. God is fully justified in whatever punishment God chooses, for God is blameless.

❑ *Psalm 51:5.* This verse means neither that conception is impure and sinful, nor that the birth was somehow sinfully illegitimate. The psalmist is claiming here that, as a weak and frail human being, he has never been without sin.

❑ *Psalm 51:16.* We can well imagine why the psalmist looked down on the atoning value of external sacrifice. If sin was part of every human striving, external sacrifice would be tainted with it as well. God wants the sinner to admit the need for God.

INDIVIDUAL LAMENTS

❑ *Psalm 51:18-19.* But, the psalmist is not suggesting a permanent end to the sacrificial system. After God's full restoration of Jerusalem, God will again welcome traditional sacrifices. These verses also bring the psalm up to the postexilic period of Israel's history, when Israel looked forward to a renewed Zion (after 587 B.C.)

DIMENSION THREE:
WHAT DOES THE BIBLE MEAN TO ME?

Psalms 39, 42, 43—The Diversity of the Psalms

In the psalms we find religious thoughts in all of their anger, love, pride, praise, joy, confusion, and hatred. Religious people are like the psalms. The psalms are written by religious people. Therefore, it is crucial for us not to avoid the turbulence and anger of Psalm 39 and rush like a deer to the cooling streams of Psalm 42 and the feeling of hope. If we avoid the anger we risk being dishonest to God.

Don't you sometimes feel like the author of Psalm 39? I know I do, and I need to admit it. But thank God, I also feel sometimes like the author of Psalms 42–43. But I cannot choose just one to study and read, because my religious life includes both.

You see, the Bible is a mirror. It reflects back to us our own images. The psalms are diverse because we are diverse. The collectors of the Bible were fortunately more honest than we. They wrestled with all facets of their humanity, and under the inspiration of God, they urge us to do the same. Thus, Psalm 39 is just as important as Psalms 42–43.

Does the diversity of the psalms frighten you or excite you? Do you find it helpful to view the Bible like this? How do you react to Psalm 39? How do you react to Psalms 42–43?

Arise to help me; look on my plight! / O Lᴏʀᴅ
God Almighty, the God of Israel (59:4-5).

9
Individual Laments

• • •

DIMENSION ONE:
WHAT DOES THE BIBLE SAY?

Answer these questions by reading Psalm 55

1. What is the psalmist's wish? (55:6-8)

2. Who is the psalmist's antagonist? (55:13)

3. What has the antagonist done? (55:20-21)

Answer these questions by reading Psalm 56

4. How does God remember the pains of the psalmist? (56:8)

5. What will the psalmist do for God? (56:12)

Answer these questions by reading Psalm 57

6. How will God save the psalmist? (57:3)

7. How are the psalmist's enemies described? (57:4)

8. What is the psalmist's response to God? (57:7)

Answer these questions by reading Psalm 58

9. What do the "rulers" do? (58:2)

10. When do wicked people become wicked? (58:3)

11. What will the righteous do when the wicked perish? (58:10)

Answer this question by reading Psalm 59

12. Should the wicked be killed? (59:11, 13)

Answer these questions by reading Psalm 69

13. How does the psalmist describe the problem? (69:1-3)

14. What has brought on the psalmist's problems? (69:9)

15. What have the comforters given to the sufferer? (69:21)

Answer this question by reading Psalm 71

16. How long has the psalmist trusted God? (71:5-6)

Answer these questions by reading Psalm 77

17. What is the psalmist's difficult question about God? (77:9)

18. How does the psalmist think to move beyond despair? (77:11-12)

19. What historic events does the psalmist remember? (77:16-20)

DIMENSION TWO:
WHAT DOES THE BIBLE MEAN?

The psalms covered in this lesson are 55, 56, 57, 59, 69, 71, and 77. Psalms 54, 58, 61, 63, 64, and 70 are of the same type, but are not looked at here.

As we begin our third lesson on the individual lament psalms, we want to look with special care at the rich diversity of insight and perspective provided in these psalms. As you read the psalms for this lesson, compare and contrast the problems they struggle with and the answers they do or do not provide for the problems raised.

❏ *Psalm 55:6-8.* After a traditional address and general complaint (verses 1-5), the psalmist, in this highly individual psalm, gives honest vent to the desire to fly away from the difficulty. Verse 6 became a reference to going to heaven after death.

❏ *Psalm 55:12-14.* The traditional view of the enemy now is given a sharply untraditional cast. If only the usual oppressive and evil enemy were involved, the psalmist could bear it. But, companion and friend has turned against the psalmist. No more painful experience can exist than when a former friend becomes estranged and antagonistic.

❏ *Psalm 55:20-21.* In sarcastic phrases, the former friend now turned enemy is attacked as a liar and deceiver.

❏ *Psalm 55:22.* Only God can help in the desperate struggle with the former friend.

The word translated "cares" is not easily understood. Some ancient translations read *love* at this point.

❏ *Psalm 56.* The title attaches this psalm to a specific event in David's life. Of the thirteen psalms so attached, eleven are laments. Psalm 34 also refers to the tale of David's false madness before Achish, king of Gath. (See 1 Samuel 21:12-15.)

❏ *Psalm 56:1.* The word *men* is more correctly "fighters" or "battlers." The remainder of the address and complaint is very familiar.

❏ *Psalm 56:8.* In this psalm God's scroll records the sufferer's problems. God will then remember them, after reading the scroll, and will requite the enemy for those tears. In Psalm 40:7, the "scroll" is a place where the psalmist is found by God to be a good person. In Psalm 139:16, the psalmist's life is recorded in the book even before his conception in the womb. That book is a kind of predestined log of life.

❏ *Psalm 56:12-13.* After some proof of God's help in the service of worship, the psalmist vows to give thank offerings to God.

❏ *Psalm 57.* The title apparently refers to the story in 1 Samuel 24. Ascribing these psalms to David at difficult moments in his life creates the picture of a man of great prayer and piety. David was a man of piety, but he was also very complex, often appearing more shrewd than pious.

❑ *Psalm 57:3.* God will shame the enemies by the gift of steadfast love and faithfulness. This response of the psalmist is quite different than the strong requests for vengeance found in Psalm 35.

❑*Psalm 57:4.* This description of the enemy is quite similar to that of Psalm 22.

❑*Psalm 57:5.* Note that this psalm, like Psalms 42–43, has a refrain, here and in verse 11.

❑*Psalm 57:7-10.* The psalmist vows a thanksgiving hymn, sung in anticipation of deliverance by God. These verses are nearly identical to Psalm 108:1-5.

❑*Psalm 58:1.* In sharp contrast to the preceding psalm, we now have this psalm of violence and hatred. The opening attack is against "rulers," literally gods who claim to control the world but do not. The remainder of the psalm is a description of the wicked who follow these false gods. The psalmist feels he is not battling against flesh and blood but against divine forces of evil that require strong measures to insure their defeat.

❑*Psalm 58:3-5.* The wicked are evil from the day they are born. Wickedness so bad as to be unchangeable is described here in an exaggerated way.

❑*Psalm 58:6-9.* The psalmist utters a curse on the wicked, perhaps to counteract a curse previously placed on the psalmist by them.

❑*Psalm 58:10-11.* When the wicked are slaughtered, the righteous will rejoice and take a bath in their blood. We ought neither to rationalize nor explain away this violence. Religious persons who simplify right and wrong often manifest their simplicity in hatred and violence. Much of history is a tragic witness to the truth of Psalm 58.

❑*Psalm 59:3-4.* The psalmist proclaims innocence. The evil ones are attacking the psalmist without cause.

❑*Psalm 59:6-7.* The enemies are pictured again in animal-like ways. They are dogs. They claim that no one will hear them as they do their evil work.

❑*Psalm 59:11-13.* A problem in the Hebrew text of verse 11 can affect the way we understand this psalm. In the NIV, the apparent command, "Do not kill them," is contradictory to verse 13. Some scholars assume verse 11 has been copied incorrectly or has been understood improperly. But the contradictory commands may represent a difficulty on the part of the psalmist in deciding which action is appropriate for God to do.

❑*Psalm 69.* This psalm does not contain predictions of Jesus, but is the psalmist's dramatic portrayal of the characteristics of suffering. For this reason the early church was attracted to it.

❑*Psalm 69:1-3.* The psalmist's distress is described in traditional water language. (See Psalms 18:16, 40:2, and Jonah 2:3 for similar phrases.)

❑*Psalm 69:7.* The psalmist presents the idea that the godly suffer for God's sake.

❑*Psalm 69:9.* This verse is quoted in two New Testament texts. In John 2:17 the disciples remember the verse as Jesus drives the moneychangers out of the Temple. The other quotation occurs in Romans 15:3. Paul is admonishing the Roman church "to bear with the failings of the weak," just as Jesus did not come to please himself but came to bear the weakness of all.

❑*Psalm 69:8-12.* The psalmist's zeal has led to estrangement from his own family and to public disgrace.

❑*Psalm 69:20.* A lovely tenor recitative and an aria from Handel's *Messiah* use this verse as a reference to the abandonment of Jesus by all those around him.

❑*Psalm 69:22-28.* The psalmist utters a lengthy curse against the enemies. These verses are reminiscent of Psalm 58:7-9.

❑*Psalm 69:35-36.* This may be a reference to the postexilic (after 587 B.C.) hope that God will rebuild the destroyed Jerusalem.

❑*Psalm 71.* This psalm was probably written by an older person. It says that age offers no escape from the wiles of enemies. Age does provide a wealth of experience that may be called upon in times of special trouble.

❑*Psalm 71:5-6.* The psalmist has always trusted in God alone from birth, and this trust is a motivation for the intervention of God.

❏*Psalm 71:9-11.* The psalmist's old age is a disadvantage when the enemies come to slander. The author's "strength is gone." Only God can now provide the needed comfort and deliverance.

❏*Psalm 71:14-16.* The psalmist, in anticipation of salvation from God, vows to praise God even more than at present.

❏*Psalm 71:20.* The psalmist is describing God's power to revive him even from the "depths of the earth," not resurrection. (See Psalms 9:13; 30:3.)

❏*Psalm 77.* Though included in our discussion of individual lament psalms, this psalm is probably a communal lament. The "I" represents the whole people.

❏*Psalm 77:5-10.* The cause of the lament is quite different from those we have seen in previous individual laments. The psalmist remembers the "good old days" with God and asks some very painful questions. Has God's steadfast love ended? Has God forgotten? Has God's compassion finally been swallowed up by anger? The problem is that God seems to have changed.

❏*Psalm 77:11-20.* Upon remembering the great deeds of God's past dealings with Israel, the psalmist appears to answer those rhetorical questions in the negative. However, this lament contains no promise to God of praise.

DIMENSION THREE:
WHAT DOES THE BIBLE MEAN TO ME?

Psalm 58—God's Vengeance

The basic meaning of vengeance in the Bible is the restoration of wholeness, of *shalom,* to the community. All talk of vengeance must be seen in that light. Our greatest obstacle to understanding the word *vengeance* is its connotation in English of vindictiveness or revenge. Very seldom in the Bible does it mean either. Vengeance is understood to be a necessary means for healing a break in the community, a break that threatens the equilibrium of God's moral order. Thus, when the psalmist cries for God's vengeance, he in reality is calling for God's healing, health, and redemption, even though they may involve retributive justice.

Even so, Psalm 58 demonstrates a ferocity and fury that cannot be avoided or explained away. Why is such a psalm here in the Bible?

Jacob Bronowski, the author of *The Ascent of Man*, feels that the horror of Auschwitz Concentration Camp and the murder of six million Jews can happen when any idea is raised to the level of dogma. (See *The Ascent of Man*, page 374.) Bronowski is referring, of course, to the inhuman and perverse idea that Jews were not really persons, they were beasts whose death was necessary. For Hitler's Germany, this astonishing idea became dogma. The result was slaughter beyond any nightmare's ability to imagine.

When the author of Psalm 58 speaks with such righteous indignation, he raises the idea of what is righteous and wicked to the level of dogma. The result is death. In both testaments the warning is sounded against any human being taking vengeance on another. God says, "It is mine to avenge" (Deuteronomy 32:35). Paul echoes the phrase in Romans 12:19. We are neither wise enough nor good enough to punish our enemies justly.

Does the Bible's talk of vengeance trouble you? How have you thought of it in the past? What does it mean for you to leave vengeance to God? In what ways are you a vengeful person?

Out of the depths
I cry to you, O LORD (130:1).

—— **10** ——

Individual Laments

• • •

DIMENSION ONE:
WHAT DOES THE BIBLE SAY?

Answer these questions by reading Psalm 88

1. Where does the psalmist draw near? (88:3)

2. Does God remember the dead? (88:5)

3. Does the psalmist have any hope? (88:13-18)

Answer these questions by reading Psalm 94

4. How is God described? (94:1)

5. What do the wicked do? (94:5-7)

6. Who rises up against the wicked? (94:17)

Answer these questions by reading Psalm 102

7. What are the days of the psalmist like? (102:3)

8. What will cause future generations to praise God? (102:19-20)

9. What will finally perish? (102:25-26)

Answer these questions by reading Psalm 108

10. Why will the psalmist sing praise? (108:4)

11. What is Moab to God? (108:9)

12. Who will trample down the psalmist's foes? (108:13)

Answer these questions by reading Psalm 109

13. What does the psalmist receive in return for love? (109:5)

14. What does the psalmist want to happen to those who curse? (109:17)

15. What is the psalmist's condition? (109:22-25)

Answer these questions by reading Psalm 120

16. Where does the psalmist live? (120:5)

17. What does the psalmist want? (120:7)

Answer these questions by reading Psalm 130

18. Where is the psalmist located? (130:1)

19. If God counted sins, who could stand? (130:3)

20. For whom should Israel hope? (130:7)

Answer these questions by reading Psalm 139

21. What has God done to the psalmist? (139:1-3)

22. Where can the psalmist flee from God's presence? (139:7-12)

23. What did God do originally for the psalmist? (139:13)

DIMENSION TWO:
WHAT DOES THE BIBLE MEAN?

The psalms covered in this lesson are 88, 94, 102, 108, 109, 120, 130, and 139. Psalms 86, 140, 141, 142, and 143 are also individual laments, but are not examined here.

❏ *Psalm 88.* In this dark psalm, the psalmist prays in vain. God provides no response, and the psalmist offers no vow. This psalm should remind us that even dark suffering is part of the reality of God and human experience.

❏ *Psalm 88:1.* The Hebrew reads "O LORD, God of my salvation," as the New Revised Standard Version (NRSV) text rightly has it. This reading makes the silence of God more awesome and terrifying as the psalmist cries to God in vain.

❏ *Psalm 88:10-12.* This psalmist does not believe in immortality. The chief characteristics of God, steadfast love and faithfulness, are not in evidence in Sheol. The psalmist seems afraid, but hopes that God will still come to deliver.

❏ *Psalm 88:15-18.* In these verses God is blamed squarely for the psalmist's agonies: loneliness, terror, helplessness. This psalm indicates a depth of isolation from God.

❏ *Psalm 94:1-3.* This psalmist's faith in the God of justice is sorely tried, and he cries out for the certainty of that justice. God must come to return the community to *shalom*. The wicked must cease their exulting.

❏ *Psalm 94:4-7.* The wicked are described in the most horrible of ways. The legal traditions of Israel demand special concern for widows, strangers, and orphans. The prophets also attack Israel for its refusal to treat these groups justly.

❑ *Psalm 94:11.* The word *futile* refers to the insubstantial quality of human beings. Here the word applies to the wicked. The NRSV presents the same thought by saying, "they are but an empty breath."

❑ *Psalm 94:12.* The psalmist draws the conclusion that suffering is a chastening by God and should be received happily. This conception of suffering as teaching is used by Job's friends. (See Job 5:17 and 36:10.)

❑ *Psalm 94:17.* "Lain down silently" is a more literal reading than the NIV translation.

❑ *Psalm 94:23.* The Hebrew word translated *destroy* in the NIV actually means to silence. Thus, God "will silence them for their wickedness."

❑ *Psalm 102:1-11.* The cry to God is bold, accusing God of "throwing the psalmist aside" (verse 10).

❑ *Psalm 102:12-22.* This long hymnic section is recited in anticipation of God's future salvation of the worshiper and perhaps for God's gift of glory to Zion (verses 21-22).

❑ *Psalm 102:23-27.* The psalmist asks God not to take him in the middle of life. But then the psalmist sees that in the broad sweep of the universe God is always the same (verse 27). In the end even the heavens will perish (verse 26).

❑ *Psalm 108.* Verses 1-5 are nearly identical to Psalm 57:7-11, and verses 6-13 are nearly identical to Psalm 60:5-12. This fact emphasizes that the psalms were used by the community of worship. They were lively and functional units of poetry that were effective and usable. Thus, two psalms were fit together to meet some given need of the community.

❑ *Psalm 108:7-9.* God now speaks through the mouth of a prophet or priest. God claims those territories that once were part of the United Monarchy at its greatest height.

❑ *Psalm 108:12-13.* The psalmist prays for victory, but asserts that only God can provide it. This may be a royal psalm of lament with the king as speaker.

❑ *Psalm 109:1-5.* The psalmist, probably accused of murder, proclaims innocence of the crime, saying that love has always been his way and the accusers only give hatred.

❑ *Psalm 109:6-19.* The accused repeats before God all the accusations uttered by the accusers. The psalmist's alleged crime probably is sorcery (verse 6).

INDIVIDUAL LAMENTS

❏ *Psalm 109:20-27.* After praying that these curses may fall on the accusers, the psalmist laments his physical condition.

❏ *Psalm 109:30-31.* Finally the psalmist praises God.

❏ *Psalm 120:1.* This verse should be translated in the past tense. Thus, the lament has already been answered, and the psalmist is here simply repeating it.

❏ *Psalm 120:2-4.* "Arrows and coals" is a metaphorical way of saying "doom and destruction."

❏ *Psalm 120:5-6.* The names of Meshech and Kedar are merely examples of remote places inhabited by wild tribes.

❏ *Psalm 120:7.* The psalmist counsels peace, but the neighbors want only war. This psalm could apply to any place where quarrels arise about peace and war, and where oaths and promises are broken.

❏ *Psalm 130.* This psalm begins with a confession of sin and moves to an acceptance of God's forgiveness.

❏ *Psalm 130:3.* If God would keep "a record of sins," that is, not forgive them, how could anyone remain alive? Of course, no one could.

❏ *Psalm 130:4.* Fortunately, God forgives sins. And for that very reason, God is to be held in awe.

❏ *Psalm 139.* This may be the most directly theological of all the psalms. However, the poet does not speak in abstract phrases about God. The psalmist prays to God in the context of real need. God's answer develops a theology that has had profound implications for all theological discussion since.

❏ *Psalm 139:1-6.* The emphasis in this section is on God's knowledge. God knows all things. Theologians call this God's omniscience. Yet, God is affirmed as omniscient because God knows the psalmist intimately. The psalmist does not spout abstract theology here, but shows how this belief was gained through personal experience.

❏ *Psalm 139:7-12.* God is everywhere. The idea that God is in "the depths" (that is, Sheol, or the grave) (verse 8) is quite startling. Up to now, this has been quite specifically denied (see Psalms 88:5-6; 115:17).

❏ *Psalm 139:17-18.* The psalmist's theological reflection concludes with the humble admission that he cannot begin to grasp all there is of God.

❏ *Psalm 139:23-24.* The psalmist concludes with a request for God to test him. The last line would be better read, "And lead me in the ancient way."

DIMENSION THREE:
WHAT DOES THE BIBLE MEAN TO ME?

Psalms 88 and 139—The God of the Psalms

These astonishingly diverse poems give us an insight into a simple fact that we must always keep in mind as we study theology. Our perception of God is just that: our perception. The author of Psalm 88 prays daily to God and hears nothing. As far as the psalmist is able to see, God does not hear or care. Further, God is cut off from Sheol and the dead, just as surely as the dead are cut off from God (88:5, 10-12). The poem ends with the wicked surrounding the isolated sufferer, ready to destroy the psalmist once and for all. What sort of God is this?

In Psalm 139, we have a very different picture. God is everywhere, knows everything, and does good works always. In a world ruled and ordered by such a God, no lasting place can be found for wickedness. Its doom is sealed. God will be triumphant everywhere and for all time.

These are two very different divine portraits from two very diverse psalmists. The author of Psalm 139 provides the reason for the diversity. Let me translate verses 17-18:

> And to me, how difficult are thoughts of you,
> > O God, how vast is their origin,
> If I would count them, they are more than sand;
> > Were I to come to the end, I would still be with you.

Even if all our thoughts of God should be numbered and stored in a computer, God would still be there, unknown and mysterious. Our thoughts of God will never end, for God is far greater than any of them.

When asked to describe God, how do you begin? Are there different ideas expressed among class members? From where do the ideas come?

By the rivers of Babylon
we sat and wept (137:1).

—— **11** ——

Communal Laments

• • •

DIMENSION ONE:
WHAT DOES THE BIBLE SAY?

Answer these questions by reading Psalm 12

1. How does the psalmist describe the rest of humanity? (12:1-2)

2. What does the psalmist hope the Lord will do? (12:3-4)

3. How does the psalmist describe God's promise? (12:6)

Answer these questions by reading Psalm 44

4. What has the psalmist heard about God? (44:1-3)

5. In what does the psalmist not trust? (44:6)

6. Why does Israel "face death all day long"? (44:22)

Answer these questions by reading Psalm 74

7. What does the psalmist ask God to remember? (74:2)

8. What have God's enemies done to the sanctuary? (74:7)

9. On what fact of God's history does the psalmist rely? (74:12-17)

Answer these questions by reading Psalm 80

10. How is God described in the first verse? (80:1)

11. How is Israel described? (80:8-13)

Answer these questions by reading Psalm 83

12. What are the enemies saying in this psalm? (83:4)

13. Which groups have made alliance against Israel? (83:6-8)

Answer these questions by reading Psalm 90

14. How long has God been God? (90:2)

15. What are one thousand years in God's sight? (90:4)

16. How long does the psalmist claim to live? (90:10)

Answer these questions by reading Psalm 126

17. What happened when the Lord brought back the captives to Zion? (126:2)

18. What does the psalmist want God to do? (126:4)

Answer these questions by reading Psalm 137

19. Where is the psalmist writing the psalm? (137:1)

20. What did the oppressors ask of the captives? (137:3)

21. What would make the psalmist happy with regard to Babylon? (137:8-9)

DIMENSION TWO:
WHAT DOES THE BIBLE MEAN?

The psalms covered in this lesson are Psalms 12, 44, 74, 80, 83, 90, 126, and 137. Psalms 60, 79, 85, 123, 125, and 129 are also communal laments, but are not examined here.

The form of the communal laments is no different from that of the individual laments. Their corporate concern sometimes makes the content of the lament different. We need to remember, however, that all the laments, whether originally communal or individual, were used by the worshiping community and were not confined to individuals praying.

❑ *Psalm 12:1.* The psalm begins with a cry of help and urges God to come, because there are no "godly " persons left. The psalmist feels lost in a world of the godless and cries to the only source of help in such a time.

❑ *Psalm 12:2.* Now the reasons the enemy are called godless are given. The godless are characterized by constant deceit. They have flattering lips, but literally "double hearts," a delightful and graphic way to express the fact that they are hypocrites.

❑ *Psalm 12:3-4.* God is called to "cut off all flattering lips and every boastful tongue." Not only are they deceitful and hypocritical, they boast that no one can judge them because they are so clever.

❑ *Psalm 12:5.* The psalmist affirms that God will rise up in defense against these smooth-tongued enemies.

❑ *Psalm 12:6.* The mention of "words of the LORD" contrasts with the "lying tongues."

❑ *Psalm 12:6-8.* Verses 6-8 are apparently the response of the community, glorifying the trustworthiness of God's words. They are confident that the lament of verses 1-4 will be heard and answered.

❑ *Psalm 44.* This communal lament begins rather like a hymn. Verses 1-3 glorify God for great past deeds and verses 4-8 provide testimony to past victories with the implied request for new victories. Verses 9-16 then list typical afflictions in the manner of a national lament. Verses 17-22 describe the religious afflictions. Verses 23-26 are a prayer for help that includes elements of lament again. This reiteration of the lament emphasizes the difficult circumstances of the defeated community at prayer.

❑ *Psalm 44:1-3.* The psalmist first recalls in a very general way the victory of the forebears of Israel and the move to the Promised Land. God gave them this victory because God loved them. On this simple phrase rests the hope of this psalmist and of Israel. God loves us.

❑ *Psalm 44:4-8.* The psalmist proclaims that the worshiping community still credits God with any victories.

❑ *Psalm 44:9-16.* The people of Israel have suffered a severe military defeat (verse 10), a sure sign that God has "rejected" them. As a result they are ashamed and debased by their conquerors (verses 13-16).

❑ *Psalm 44:17-22.* The psalmist here rejects the claim that God has forgotten the people because they have forgotten God. They have done all for God's sake, and have prayed only to God (verse 20). Paul quotes verse 22 in his poem to the inseparable love of God in Romans 8:36.

❑ *Psalm 44:23-26.* The final plea is desperate and heartfelt. The community in defeat is in real need.

❑ *Psalm 74.* This lament for the destruction of the Temple does not necessarily refer to the great destruction by Babylon in 587 B.C. or to the Temple's desecration by Antiochus IV in 167 B.C. It could refer to any time in the Temple's life when it was threatened.

❑ *Psalm 74:1-3.* The devastation of the Temple brings on a crisis of belief. The psalmist asks the question, If God's Temple is destroyed, then where is God and why did God not stop this sacrilege?

❑ *Psalm 74:4-8.* The destruction is now described. Not only did the foes destroy the Temple itself, they also burned all the meeting places of God. The attempt to obliterate the worship of God is nearly complete.

❑ *Psalm 74:9-11.* Because the Temple is gone, there appear to be no signs of God's presence anymore.

❑ *Psalm 74:12-17.* The cultic community now recites a list of God's great powers as creator of the universe, referring to the ancient story of the defeat of chaos to form the universe. (See page 35 for the discussion of Psalm 89.)

❑ *Psalm 74:18-23.* Now that God's power has been affirmed again, the community urges God to manifest power in this new chaos by pleading God's cause against the fool.

❑ *Psalm 80.* This psalm has often been connected with the last days of the Northern Kingdom, Israel. During the final days, the community assembled to lament its fate. The Northern Kingdom was annihilated in 721 B.C. by the Assyrians.

❑ *Psalm 80:1-3.* The God of past shepherding is called upon for aid. The tribes listed were always identified with northern Israel. The refrain, "make your face shine upon us, / that we may be saved," is repeated in verses 7 and 19. It may have been a congregational response to the laments of the leaders of worship.

❑ *Psalm 80:4-7.* The community expresses its crisis of belief, because of the defeat by its enemies.

❑ *Psalm 80:8-13.* The metaphor of Israel as a vine is a vivid and powerful one. (See Genesis 49:22; Hosea 10:1; Jeremiah 2:21; Isaiah 5:1-7.)

❑ *Psalm 80:14-19.* Protection for the vine is asked for again. The psalmist claims that "we will not turn away from you."

❑ *Psalm 83:1-2.* Here the psalmist calls on God. Not only do the enemies hate the psalmist, they hate God as well.

❑ *Psalm 83:3-8.* The nation draws together in worship under the belief that all other nations are enemies who have allied together to destroy them.

❑ *Psalm 90.* Despite the title of this psalm, it is definitely not an old one. Its concern for God to grant happiness to the individual during a short and transient life is an interest raised by a community that has been around for a while.

❑ *Psalm 90:1.* The phrase, "Lord, you have been our dwelling place / throughout all generations" sets the theological framework for this psalm. God always has been and always will be our refuge and home.

❑ *Psalm 90:2-6.* Now the psalmist turns to the sharp contrast between God's eternal existence and human mortality.

❑ *Psalm 90:7-12.* Humans are mortal because while God rules they attempt to dislodge that rule.

COMMUNAL LAMENTS   **93**

❑ *Psalm 90:13-17.* The prayer ends with the supplication to God that God will provide grace and allow them to "sing for joy and be glad all our days" (verse 14).

❑ *Psalm 126.* This psalm was probably written and used in the time of Judah's (the Southern Kingdom's) exile (after 587 B.C.).

❑ *Psalm 126:1.* Present tense would seem more appropriate. "We were like men who dreamed" seems to be a reference to new hope. After God restores Zion, new hope will ensue.

❑ *Psalm 126:2.* Joy and laughter will be prevalent, with the implication that such is not the case now. Even the Gentiles ("the nations") will admit that God has done great things for them.

❑ *Psalm 137:1-3.* The Judahites (from the Southern Kingdom of Judah) are in exile in Babylon. They fondly and longingly remember Zion and, as a result, hang their harps on the trees, a symbol that they could not praise God in such an evil land. But the enemy requires a song of Zion to mock them and taunt them in their anguish.

❑ *Psalm 137:4.* They claim that God's song cannot be sung in a foreign land.

❑ *Psalm 137:5-6.* Only Jerusalem has meaning for the people of Judah. Only there can they sing and praise. But Jerusalem is gone.

❑ *Psalm 137:7-9.* The Edomites apparently took advantage of the Babylonian destruction of Jerusalem by joining in the general looting that followed (see Obadiah, verse 11). The psalmist then turns on the Babylonians and utters one of the Bible's most terrible phrases, rivaling even the horror of Psalm 58.

DIMENSION THREE:
WHAT DOES THE BIBLE MEAN TO ME?

Psalms 74, 83, and 137—Responses to Crisis

The psalms provide a fascinating look at severe crises of faith and life and at which kinds of responses are made to those crises. Let us look again at three of the psalms of this lesson.

Psalm 74 records the shattering tragedy of the destruction of the Jerusalem Temple. The Temple served as the focal point of much Israelite worship for nearly 450 years, from its construction by Solomon about 950 B.C., to its destruction by the Babylonians in 587 B.C. God was thought to be uniquely present in the Temple in Jerusalem.

The author of Psalm 74, in the face of the Temple's demise, does not only despair. In 74:12-17, the psalmist turns to a recital of God's creative power even though the great Temple has been destroyed. In other words, the psalmist was able to go beyond the building to see the power of God. Thus, the end of the psalm can expect the action of God who is not confined to any building.

In Psalm 83, the psalmist is confronted, in his mind, by a terrible conspiracy of evil. The psalmist feels all nations are against Israel. As a result, great hatred is poured out on them by the author as God's curse is demanded to destroy them. When it is "us" against "them," great hatred can only be the result.

Great hatred is also obvious in Psalm 137. The psalmist is exiled in the enemy country of Babylonia. The exiles all long nostalgically for Jerusalem. They cannot find a way to sing the Lord's song in a foreign land. As a result, they can only cry out for the death and obliteration of their enemies. The problem is obvious. If they cannot adapt to a new situation and can only find meaning in a situation long past, they are bound to become frustrated and hostile toward those who caused these new circumstances.

Here then are three responses to crisis in the communal laments. Psalm 74 goes beyond despair to hope in God's power; Psalm 83 draws for us a caricature of the enemy and ends in hatred; Psalm 137 longs for a lost past and is thus led to desire death for those who caused the loss. How do you respond to a crisis in your life? Do these psalms provide insight concerning how to respond or how not to respond? How does your faith help you in a crisis?

—— 12 ——
Wisdom Psalms
• • •

DIMENSION ONE:
WHAT DOES THE BIBLE SAY?

Answer these questions by reading Psalm 1

1. How can a person be blessed? (1:1-2)

2. How does the psalm describe this happy one? (1:3)

3. What are the wicked like? (1:4)

Answer these questions by reading Psalm 37

4. Why should we not worry about the wicked? (37:2)

5. Why should we have patience? (37:10)

6. Where does the salvation of the righteous come from? (37:39)

Answer these questions by reading Psalm 49

7. Who is addressed in the psalm? (49:1-2)

8. Why should we not fear those who trust only in wealth? (49:7-9)

9. From where will God ransom the psalmist? (49:15)

Answer these questions by reading Psalm 73

10. Why did the psalmist have feelings of envy? (73:3)

11. How did the psalmist regain true faith in God? (73:17)

12. How does the psalmist describe himself? (73:22)

Answer these questions by reading Psalm 78

13. How does the psalmist propose to speak? (78:2)

WISDOM PSALMS

14. How does the psalmist describe the forebears of Israel? (78:8)

15. What is God's last act recounted in the psalm? (78:70)

Answer these questions by reading Psalm 91

16. Who is the person who is safe from peril? (91:1)

17. How will God guard your ways? (91:11)

18. How will the psalmist know that God has given salvation? (91:16)

Answer these questions by reading Psalm 127

19. Who must always build the house? (127:1)

20. Is rising early and going to bed late helpful? (127:2)

21. What makes a person happy? (127:4)

22. How should brothers live? (133:1)

23. What is the unity of brothers like? (133:2)

DIMENSION TWO:
WHAT DOES THE BIBLE MEAN?

The wisdom psalms are Psalms 1, 37, 49, 73, 78, 91, 112, 127, and 133. Psalms 119 and 128 are also wisdom psalms, but are not examined here.

❏ *Psalm 1.* It is significant that the entire Book of Psalms begins with this one. The basic question this psalm raises is about the identity and fate of the righteous and the wicked. Just who is righteous and who is wicked? The psalms as a whole address this question and give many and varied answers, as we have seen.

❏ *Psalm 1:1-3.* That person is happy (NIV "blessed") who does not "walk" or "stand" or "sit" in any place where the wicked do. The active verbs seem to imply that the wicked are always busy with their wickedness. In contrast, the happy one is the one who "meditates," a purposely inactive verb. This person's delight is in God's *torah* ("law").

❏ *Psalm 1:4-5.* But the wicked are described in a contrasting image. They are like chaff, that useless material that is separated from the grain by throwing the crushed sheaves in the air where the wind can automatically separate chaff from grain. The "judgment" of verse 5 is not some afterlife tribunal. The parallel line refers to the congregation, and thus tells us that the judgment is a this-worldly one that determines who can remain in the worshiping community.

❏ *Psalm 37.* This psalm is a collection of proverb-like sections. These parts are strung together as an acrostic poem with every other line beginning with a successive letter of the Hebrew alphabet. The psalm has no consistent thought movement, given the artificial structure of the acrostic. But it has a very simple point. The author wants to guide the readers into a true confidence of God.

❏ *Psalm 37:1-7.* The title of this psalm might just as well be "Do not worry about things that are hard to comprehend." The wicked? They will fade like grass (verse 2). The evil? Be patient and still before God (verse 7).

❏ *Psalm 37:8-22.* The wicked are terrible. The psalmist says again and again that they will perish (verses 10, 13, 17, 20, 22).

❏ *Psalm 37:34.* The psalmist here seems to reject the probing questions of earlier lament psalms. "Wait for the LORD"; do not complain about the wicked. Just wait, and you will see their fall. We find in this psalm no theoretical analysis of the problem of evil. The psalm is more pastoral than intellectual. "Do this," it says, "and you will live."

❏ *Psalm 49.* This interesting psalm addresses one of life's oldest riddles. How do we deal with persons of wealth and influence who seem to have control over our lives?

❏ *Psalm 49:1-4.* The psalmist calls everyone to witness how he has solved the riddle. The problem is seen as one to be solved by the intellect with the guidance of faith.

❏ *Psalm 49:5-6.* Here the main problem is stated. Why should the psalmist fear when wealthy, boasting persecutors are all around? The implication is that once fear was common in such a time. But apparently the psalmist has found a way to conquer the fear.

❏ *Psalm 49:7-12.* First, in beginning a solution to the problem, the psalmist states two negative facts. Verses 7-9 affirm that no one buys his or her way out of death. There is not enough money in the world to buy life. Verses 10-12 claim that all persons die, whether wise or foolish, rich or poor (compare Ecclesiastes 3:19-20.

❏ *Psalm 49:13-15.* The psalmist now contrasts the harsh fate of the wicked (verses 13-14) with the assurance that God will save the psalmist from this present trouble. Many have read verse 15 as the psalmist's assurance of a personal immortality. However, the verse probably refers to present trouble rather than life after death.

❑ *Psalm 73.* This psalm is the product of a major conflict in the thought of the Old Testament. The psalm is far more than an intellectual exercise. It is fully a question of life and death, a question of the survival of faith.

❑ *Psalm 73:1-3.* The psalmist starts the psalm by mentioning the belief that nearly disappeared in the midst of the struggle the psalm records. The feet of the psalmist had almost stumbled and slipped due to the glaring reality of the prosperity of the wicked.

❑ *Psalm 73:4-16.* These verses record that wicked prosperity in the most graphic of pictures. The wicked are comfortable, rich, arrogant, and praised. On the contrary, the psalmist, though clean and innocent, is stricken all day long. The psalmist tried to comprehend this terrible truth, but it seemed to be "oppressive" and finally insoluble.

❑ *Psalm 73:17.* The psalm's turning point occurs when the psalmist enters the sanctuary of God and is granted a revelation about the end of the wicked.

❑ *Psalm 73:18-28.* The psalmist now knows that the wicked are doomed. For the psalmist to doubt that truth was to be stupid and ignorant. Also, the psalmist is now convinced that God is strength and refuge forever.

❑ *Psalm 78.* This psalm relies heavily on history for its content. Other psalms are also concerned with history (Psalms 77, 105, and 106). But those psalms deal with the history of Israel in a quite different way from Psalm 78. History is for this psalmist "hidden things, things from of old" (verse 2). This psalm claims that history is often irrational. That is, history moves in ways we can hardly anticipate.

❑ *Psalm 78:1-8.* The psalm is introduced in the way wisdom psalms usually begin, by referring to the contents as a parable and as *torah*. The psalm is uttered so that future generations will always remember God's nature and purpose (verse 5). But the readers are warned never to forget human sin. Be faithful (verse 7), but be warned against being stubborn and rebellious (verse 8).

WISDOM PSALMS

❏ *Psalm 78:9-33.* The psalm argues that the tribe of Joseph (represented by Ephraim in verse 9) had received the covenant and was an eyewitness to God's mighty deeds in the Exodus from Egypt (verse 11). This tribe also received God's law at Sinai but would not keep it (verse 10). Verses 12-33 of this psalm record the continual rejection by the tribe of Joseph of God's activity in the desert.

❏ *Psalm 78:54-60.* Even after the gift of the Promised Land, the people still rebelled. So God "rejected Israel" (verse 59). God demonstrated that rejection by destroying Shiloh, a sacred place of worship (verse 60).

❏ *Psalm 78:67-72.* Now the reason for the psalm's long, sordid tale becomes clear. God rejected Joseph, the chief tribe of the northern part of Israel. But God chose Judah, which resides on Mount Zion in Jerusalem. The chief figure of the tribe of Judah is of course, David, God's servant (verse 70). Thus, the entire psalm is a lengthy meditation on why the southern Judah tribe was chosen as supreme as opposed to the northern Joseph tribe. The psalm is also didactic. It emphasizes that faithfulness and obedience are crucial to maintain a relationship to God.

❏ *Psalm 91.* This psalm is a meditation on the protection of God and human faithfulness to God.

❏ *Psalm 91:3-10.* Vivid images of God's amazing protection are provided. God is said to have feathers and wings, the image of a great sheltering bird. (See Exodus 19:4 for a similar image of God.) The terrors include war (verse 5) and illness (verse 6). But the psalmist will be safe, because he has made God shelter and refuge.

❏ *Psalm 91:11-12.* These are famous lines for Christians. They are quoted during the temptation of Jesus as recorded in Matthew 4:6 and Luke 4:10-11.

❏ *Psalm 91:14-16.* The promise of refuge is confirmed here by words of divine assurance. These words are uttered in the first person perhaps by a prophet or priest of the sanctuary. This wisdom poem, unlike some of the others we have seen, seems clearly to have been adapted for use in worship.

❏ *Psalm 127.* We might call this psalm a proverb psalm. It contains two proverbial ideas loosely connected to each other.

❑ *Psalm 127:1-2.* Here is a proverbial affirmation of divine providence in human life. Human efforts apart from God are vain. Unless God is involved in work, the work is empty and fruitless.

❑ *Psalm 127:3-5.* The second proverbial idea is that sons are an inheritance from God. This section praises the family as God's gift and as the foundation for protection against enemies. The two sections of this psalm are bound together by the thought that God is involved in the affairs of humanity: from building, to general work, to the gift of families. God permeates life.

❑ *Psalm 133.* This psalm is based on a wisdom saying, How good and pleasant it is when brothers dwell together. The word *brother* here does not mean something general about how all humanity is related. It literally means brothers in the family unit. The unity of the family was apparently a serious problem for the community of this psalmist.

❑ *Psalm 133:2.* The unity of brothers is compared to two familiar though perhaps unusual images. To us, oil dripping from a beard may have little to recommend it. But to the Israelite, the long full beard was a chief sign of manliness. And the beard of Aaron, the high priest, has special sanctity and unusual length. The law forbids it to be cut at all (Leviticus 21:5). Also, oil was a very precious substance in the ancient world. So the portrait of dripping, exquisite oil would be the height of luxury and beauty. So is the unity of brothers.

❑ *Psalm 133:3.* The fresh morning dew on Mount Hermon, the lovely snow-capped peak in the far north of Israel, is matched by the dew on Zion in Jerusalem. Dew is a symbol of cleanliness, newness, freshness, and quiet beauty.

DIMENSION THREE:
WHAT DOES THE BIBLE MEAN TO ME?

The central subject of the wisdom psalms is the question that has confronted all religious human beings throughout the centuries. Why do the wicked prosper? There is not a quick answer to that awesome question. But we can see the various answers that these wisdom psalms have provided.

Why Do the Wicked Prosper?

Let us compare and contrast the answers to our question given in Psalms 37, 49, and 73. Psalm 37 seems to give the answer, "Do not be concerned, because the wicked really do get punished." Verse 25 summarizes this answer.

On the surface, this answer is so contrary to reality that it is absurd. Any one of us can name examples that demonstrate the falseness of such a simple-minded statement. This psalmist tries to solve the problem by saying that there is no problem. This answer is, in the long run, unsatisfactory to most of us.

Psalm 49 has a different approach. We should not fear the wicked nor their riches, because death comes to all and you surely cannot take it with you. Why fear such ephemeral, transient things such as human beings, no matter how wicked they may be? Because all die, we need not be afraid. The wicked may prosper, but never for long. Is this a helpful answer for you?

Psalm 73 moves in another direction. The psalmist had nearly abandoned faith in the face of the prosperity of the wicked. But a worship service provided the satisfying answer that the wicked are eventually rewarded. This is the old answer, but it comes in the midst of worship. Is this answer useful for your thinking?

You are not going to solve this riddle today in your class. First try to understand the answers of these psalms. Then ask if the question is an important one for you and how you have wrestled with it in the past. Share your thinking with the class.

The LORD is my shepherd,
I shall not be in want (23:1).

—— 13 ——
Psalms of Confidence

• • •

DIMENSION ONE:
WHAT DOES THE BIBLE SAY?

Answer these questions by reading Psalm 11

1. What is the advice given to the psalmist? (11:1)

2. Does the psalmist accept the advice? (11:4)

3. What will God do to the wicked? (11:6)

Answer these questions by reading Psalm 16

4. What does the psalmist refuse to do? (16:4)

5. Why is the psalmist's heart glad? (16:10)

Answer these questions by reading Psalm 23

6. How is God described in the psalm? (23:1)

7. Why does God lead in the paths of righteousness? (23:3)

8. Who witnesses God's table preparation for the psalmist? (23:5)

Answer these questions by reading Psalm 131

9. What has the psalmist not done? (131:1)

10. What is the psalmist's mood? (131:2)

Answer these questions by reading Psalm 50

11. Who does God want to gather? (50:5)

12. Does God desire Israel's animal sacrifices? (50:9-13)

13. What is the sacrifice that honors God? (50:23)

Answer these questions by reading Psalm 68

14. What does the psalmist hope happens to the wicked? (68:2)

15. How is God best known in the psalm? (68:5)

16. How can one escape death? (68:20)

Answer these questions by reading Psalm 81

17. How should God be praised? (81:1-3)

18. What does God specifically reject? (81:9)

19. What would happen if Israel would listen to God? (81:14)

Answer these questions by reading Psalm 82

20. Where is God in the psalm? (82:1)

21. What is wrong with the other gods? (82:1-2)

22. Does the psalm deny the existence of other gods? (82:6-7)

DIMENSION TWO: WHAT DOES THE BIBLE MEAN?

This last lesson includes a small category that comprises five psalms, the psalms of confidence. These are Psalms 11, 16, 23, 62, and 131. The category seems to be an expansion of the expressions of trust that are characteristic of the lament psalms. (See Psalms 3:3-4; 5:3-7; 7:12-16.) Psalm 62 will not be examined here.

Also in this lesson we include four psalms that do not fit readily into any formal grouping. These are Psalms 50, 68, 81, and 82. All are apparently liturgies for special Temple use.

❑ *Psalm 11.* The major dispute of the psalms, that between righteous and wicked, forms the background for this psalm. The psalmist has found refuge in God, while others counsel flight to the mountains. But the poet resolves to face the wicked, who in any case will be destroyed by Yahweh.

❑ *Psalm 11:1-3.* To the psalmist who has found confidence and refuge in Yahweh, the advice to "flee like a bird to your mountain" is perhaps a bit insulting. Those who offer the advice demonstrate their own fear of the wicked by describing the actions of the wicked as dangerous and terrible. When the very basis of life is destroyed, what more can one do than flee?

❑ *Psalm 11:4-7.* But the psalmist reminds these timid ones that God is in the holy Temple, in the sky, observing and noting human beings. As a result, the wicked will die from "fiery coals and burning sulfur." The psalmist's refuge in God rests on this belief in the ultimate evil fate of the wicked.

❑ *Psalm 16.* Unfortunately, in this psalm a poor Hebrew text has led to a wide variety of opinions concerning the basic meaning. The key statement appears in verse 4 where other gods and their worshiping rites are rejected. The setting of the psalm is in worship where God's presence is most readily found.

❏ **Psalm 16:1-4.** As in Psalm 11, the psalm opens with the claim that the psalmist takes refuge in God. Others are apparently turning to worship other gods. The psalmist refuses to participate in some blood-rites that involve uttering divine names other than Yahweh. The psalmist's confidence and trust in Yahweh will not permit any other worship.

❏ **Psalm 16:5-8.** Having proclaimed communion with God to the exclusion of other gods, the psalmist uses the terms "portion," "cup," and "lot" to emphasize that intimate communion. This worshiper is forever connected to God; God plays an intimate part in life. The poet keeps "the LORD always before me" (verse 8). Thus, the other gods are further rejected, as God is praised as the one who gives counsel (verse 7).

❏ **Psalm 16:9-11.** As a result of this tremendous confidence in God, the psalmist bursts into praise. Verse 10 has sometimes been read as a veiled reference to resurrection or at least to a belief in immortality. However, the psalmist is probably less interested in death or afterlife than in God's ability to make death a non-fearsome idea. The psalmist is secure (verse 9) precisely because death is no longer terrifying.

❏ **Psalm 23.** This is the most familiar psalm in the Psalter. A great many persons can recite the King James Version of this psalm from memory.

❏ **Psalm 23:1-3.** The poem is deceptively simple. It is obvious that the metaphor sustained throughout is that of shepherd and sheep. Yet we never doubt that it is the psalmist who is praying a prayer that we can readily make our own. Notice how spare and brief the words are. In Hebrew, verse 1 is four words, "Yahweh is my shepherd; I do not lack."

❏ **Psalm 23:4.** The usual translation "valley of the shadow of death" should read "glen of gloom" or "the darkest valley" (see the NIV text note). The word that was thought to be "shadow of death" is a familiar image from the Canaanite culture that means "deep darkness." Certainly the poem's early hearers would have understood it so. In the face of the most profound trouble, the psalmist need not fear, for the divine shepherd is available.

❏ **Psalm 23:5.** Now the divine shepherd becomes a gracious host, who prepares a table in the midst of enemies. This image seems to suggest the calm certainty of verse 4. Even surrounded by enemies the psalmist can eat without fear, anointed with precious oil and sampling an overflowing cup, both signs of ease and luxury.

❑ *Psalm 23:6.* The psalmist wants to praise God in the sanctuary ("God's house") for as long as the psalmist lives. The familiar reading "forever" is not accurate. As long as the psalmist is able, he will go to God's house to thank God for the wonderful and certain safety and rest.

❑ *Psalm 131.* Here is the briefest of the psalms of trust. It is a marvelous statement of humility and patience, far removed from the stormy demands of the laments we have examined. The poet begins by denying any aspirations to greatness. Nor does the psalmist pursue great things that are too awesome and marvelous.

"But I have stilled and quieted my soul" (verse 2). How different from the anguish and outcries of the laments! The psalmist gives a lovely metaphor of peace and calm—like a nursing child at the breast. That is a wonderful scene to witness and perfectly apt for the psalmist's interest.

In verse 3 the psalm is adapted for the community at worship. The psalmist transfers his experience to the whole nation. Just as the poet learned to await God in humbleness and quiet, so Israel should await Yahweh. This psalm is little known but should be better known.

We turn now to four miscellaneous poems, all of which seem to have some liturgical character, but which fit no familiar literary category.

❑ *Psalm 50.* This psalm is a divine rebuke against Israel for overestimating the value of sacrifice in the worship of God. Psalms 40, 51, and 69 share this view, and many of the great prophets do, also. (See Amos 5:21-24; Isaiah 1:13-16; Micah 6:6-8.)

❑ *Psalm 50:1-6.* God is described as coming in power, precisely to judge the peoples on the basis of the covenant by sacrifice (verse 5).

❑ *Psalm 50:7-21.* Here is the divine rebuke that is divided into two sections. In the first, verses 7-15, God does not reject Israel simply because of sacrifices, a fact stated explicitly in verse 8.

110   PSALMS

But God will accept no more sacrifices from the people, because they are confused about the meaning of such activity. What God desires is heartfelt praise and completed vows (verse 14).

In the second section of the divine rebuke, God denies worship to all wicked persons. They cannot recite nor proclaim God's covenant.

❏ *Psalm 50:22-23.* The psalm closes with warning and threat (verse 22) and a promise of salvation to those who bring thanksgiving to God (verse 23). This psalm has many affinities with prophetic rebukes of the people of Israel.

❏ *Psalm 68.* This is the most difficult of all psalms to understand. The Hebrew text is very poor, and the psalm is disjointed. It is almost as if we have received a part of a liturgy, but the setting for the whole liturgy has been lost.

❏ *Psalm 68:1-3.* The opening lines point to the appearance of God who is asked to disperse and destroy the enemies.

❏ *Psalm 68:4-6.* The congregation is called upon to praise God. God is uniquely concerned with orphans, widows, the desolate, and prisoners—familiar concerns to us by now.

❏ *Psalm 68:7-10.* Now a hymn to Yahweh borrows old material from Judges 5:4 but changes it in several ways.

❏ *Psalm 68:11-23.* Many historical allusions, some unknown and some well-known, appear in this section. All these allusions show God's appearance in power to the worshipers.

❏ *Psalm 68:24-27.* The connection of the psalm to worship is clearest here. The musical procession into the sanctuary is given a vivid description.

❏ *Psalm 68:28-35.* The psalm closes with the assurance of God's final victory over all nations and a final recognition of God's universality (verses 32-35).

❏ *Psalm 81:1-5.* This part of the psalm calls the community to celebrate a feast with shouts of joy, songs, and music. The call seems especially urgent; perhaps the pressure of the enemies is very real (verse 14).

❏ *Psalm 81:6-10.* Now the word of God is given in the midst of the feast. The prophet or priest announces God's great deeds of the past—Sinai (verse 7), the desert (verse 7), the Exodus (verse 10). These deeds are not announced for their own sake.

Just as God has acted in the past with past worshipers so God will act again with these worshipers.

❏ *Psalm 81:11-16.* But the danger of the people's refusal to listen, just as their forebears refused, is great. If they would only listen, God would soon act on their behalf against their enemies. Even those who hate God would eventually flatter God. They would live long lives.

❏ *Psalm 82.* Here is a fascinating psalm that provides a powerful mythological portrait of God taking authority in heaven and on earth. God deposes the lesser gods to whom God had given some authority for a brief time. However, they forfeited that authority, and God made them mortal. So they are no longer gods.

❏ *Psalm 82:1.* The picture of God striding into the divine court of lesser gods is a vivid one. (See 1 Kings 22:19; Job 1:6; 2:1 for other pictures of a divine court of gods.)

❏ *Psalm 82:2-7.* God now deposes these lesser gods, because they have failed to execute justice on earth. For their failure they are made mortal. They will die like any human.

❏ *Psalm 82:8.* And so the community now requests justice from the only source from which it can ever come—God alone.

DIMENSION THREE:
WHAT DOES THE BIBLE MEAN TO ME?

The Use of the Psalms in Worship

Although we have no clear biblical evidence, we can be fairly certain that the psalms were used regularly in ancient Israel's worship services. Think about the worship services in your church. When are the psalms used in these services? Think about the creative ways the psalms could be used in your Sunday morning church services. Share your ideas with other class members.